What People Are Saying About Financial Finesse and *Money Strong*

One of the stark lessons from the Covid-19 pandemic was how unprepared so many Americans were for a financial emergency, such as an unexpected job loss, and how crucial financial literacy is to workers and their families. Liz Davidson is here to save the day with her inspirational and approachable book, *Money Strong*. Based on her more than 20 years of financial coaching, the book's START™ framework maps out five keys to success that anyone can employ to build the life of their dreams. With a coach like Liz Davidson on your side, how could you lose?

—MARY BETH FRANKLIN, *InvestmentNews*

With deep insights into *why* we behave with money the way we do along with actionable steps to improve, there is something for everyone in *Money Strong*. Full of success stories from real people that will motivate and inspire, this framework is proven to work. I couldn't put it down! This book will change lives.

—KELLEY C. LONG, CPA/PFS, CFP®, and personal finance speaker, writer, and coach and contributing writer, *TheStreet*

Financial Finesse's financial coaching program has changed my life in ways I never could have imagined. I have paid down all my credit card and student loan debt, have a strong 401K balance, am on track to pay for college for my children, own both of my cars outright, have bought a home, and am beginning to save for another . . . all things that I have in my life now that I did not have before I began the coaching program.

—THOMAS B, 32

I really value the wise counsel I find at Financial Finesse. By far, it is my favorite benefit.

—MIKE M, 64

If I didn't have Financial Finesse, I don't know where I would be. I wasn't in a place where I could have paid for a financial advisor. I had so much stress for so long. I've paid off my credit card debt and private loans and it just created so much more space and reduced mental strain.

—ED C, 33

It's about the team you build . . . I've been fortunate to find that environment professionally and personally . . . and Financial Finesse has been excellent coaches in building that team. . . . It's those early steps in financial security that really matter.

—AARON L, 30

Try it! You won't regret it. There are a lot of tools and resources to help you with your personal finances. I've told coworkers to try it. I teach my sister what I learn.

—ROBERLINE B, 23

I didn't realize there were times where I would just leave things up to chance because I had no one to go to. Since I've had access to Financial Finesse and their coaches, I have reached out several times on important topics for me and my family. The fact I can call a pro anytime about my finances brings me so much peace of mind!

—BILL C, 30

Sanity. Financial Finesse has given me sanity by quickly answering all the confounding questions that come up with finances.

—DOUG B, 71

I very much appreciate this coaching model. The ability to reach out to a professional for an ongoing, multiyear conversation about our personal financial strategy has been fantastic.

—AMY B, 46

It feels good to have someone to celebrate my accomplishments with and to know my financial coach is rooting for me from the sidelines.

—MARY H, 38

MONEY
STRONG

YOUR GUIDE TO A LIFE
FREE OF FINANCIAL WORRIES

LIZ DAVIDSON

NEW YORK   CHICAGO   SAN FRANCISCO   ATHENS   LONDON
MADRID   MEXICO CITY   MILAN   NEW DELHI
SINGAPORE   SYDNEY   TORONTO

1 2 3 4 5 6 7 8 9   LCR   28 27 26 25 24 23

ISBN   978-1-264-98907-2
MHID   1-264-98907-5

e-ISBN   978-1-264-98941-6
e-MHID   1-264-98941-5

This publication is designed to provide accurate and authoritative information in regard to the subject matter covered. It is sold with the understanding that neither the author nor the publisher is engaged in rendering legal, accounting, securities trading, or other professional services. If legal advice or other expert assistance is required, the services of a competent professional person should be sought.
—*From a Declaration of Principles Jointly Adopted by a Committee of the American Bar Association and a Committee of Publishers and Associations*

McGraw Hill books are available at special quantity discounts to use as premiums and sales promotions or for use in corporate training programs. To contact a representative, please visit the Contact Us pages at www.mhprofessional.com.

McGraw Hill is committed to making our products accessible to all learners. To learn more about the available support and accommodations we offer, please contact us at accessibility@mheducation.com. We also participate in the Access Text Network (www.accesstext.org), and ATN members may submit requests through ATN.

Please note that several of the names and personal details of people profiled in this book have been changed in order to protect their identities.

This book is dedicated to Jan Davidson and Doris Casale, who each in her own way fully lived her purpose and inspired me and countless others to do the same.

We collectively stand on the shoulders of our role models and mentors in life, and we in turn become the shoulders to stand on for those we inspire. While this book is designed to help you reduce your financial stress and reach financial freedom, it's also about paying the lessons forward once you do. In that vein, Financial Finesse, the financial coaching company I built to help employees become more financially secure through employer-paid financial coaching programs, is using half the proceeds received from the sale of this book to support the expansion of a philanthropic initiative we have created to ensure future generations are well-equipped to manage their finances, regardless of the challenges they inherit. This initiative is being used to deliver free financial education to college students, with a focus on student athletes who can make money from their name, image, and likeness (NIL), but who currently lack the financial coaching needed to effectively manage this opportunity. These athletes, who often come from humble beginnings and attend college on scholarship, are at a crossroads right now. With proper financial guidance and coaching, they can use their NIL earnings to get a head start in life, and potentially begin to create generational wealth. Absent this guidance, many will spend most or all of their earnings and end up owing more in taxes than they can afford to pay, putting them in significant financial jeopardy.

These student athletes are also the role models for their generation, with a collective 50 million followers on social media. The messages they send resonate and can create a ripple effect for their peers. The examples they give when it comes to money will set the tone for an entire generation to follow.

By buying this book, you are not only helping yourself, but also helping those in the next generation get the support they need to progress financially.

CONTENTS

MODULE 3

ADVANCE TOWARD THE LIFE YOU WANT

MODULE 4

ROLE MODEL GOOD FINANCIAL HABITS AND BEHAVIORS

MODULE 5

THRIVE BY LIVING YOUR PURPOSE

FOREWORD

Financial stress is real. You'd think that as an NFL player who grew up in the suburbs of Philadelphia and went to private school, I would have had the picture-perfect life, financially speaking, but that wasn't the case. Let's just say, financial stress always had a seat at the table from the time I was a kid into young adulthood. Money, through both good times and bad, has always defined the course of my life. For that reason, I've become a huge advocate of financial coaching and will remain a fan for the rest of my life. I've lived on both sides of this money equation and want to see as many people as possible become free of financial stress and get to the other side.

Here's my story:

Out of necessity, at 18, I became fully independent from my parents financially and had to figure out how to support myself. As you can probably imagine, like most 18-year-olds, I didn't have a clue how to manage this responsibility. I got myself into a situation in college where I was one day away from dropping out of Penn State because there was no way to pay my tuition. Fortunately, I received an athletic scholarship right before the fall semester of 2013. But even then, I wasn't free. The scholarship covered tuition and room and board, but not all the other expenses that come from life as a college student, like books, gas for transportation, and meals that weren't provided by the team; and of course I had to figure out how to support myself through the summer months. Even working crazy hours at odd jobs over the summer, there was always a shortfall where I had to make tough decisions about how to pay the bills. One winter break, my roommates and I forgot to shut off the water, so multiple pipes burst in our old house in downtown State College. We failed to follow the clear instructions for shutting off the water, so we were left footing the bill. I was so broke I had to sell my textbooks to come up with my share of the repairs. There was always anxiety like this, that feeling that I was never going to get out of scrambling to make ends meet.

My solution was to work what amounted to about 80 hours a week (between football and studying) to build myself a better future. I decided to throw myself into working overtime at football practice with the hope of making it in the NFL, then study like crazy to be pre-med in case football didn't work out, knowing that either way, I would ONE DAY not have to think about money. I would ONE DAY not have to buy the cheapest food at the grocery store (not necessarily a good strategy for an athlete needing real nutrition) and could walk in there and buy whatever I wanted without worrying about having enough in the bank at that moment to afford it. I would ONE DAY be able to confront the cost of a pipe repair, or any financial emergency for that matter, paying the bill on the spot and moving on without frantically searching for a way to get the money needed to cover the bill. I would ONE DAY be able to have that life I always envisioned, where I could comfortably provide for children of my own, giving them opportunities without a thought about the cost, knowing that I was OK—that I had enough.

Turns out, I was one of the incredibly lucky ones—my plan actually worked! I got drafted, and suddenly I didn't have to worry about spending too much on food, as I was making what, by anyone's standards, is a very large salary.

You've probably heard all your life that money doesn't buy happiness. And there's a lot of truth to that saying. Money in and of itself is actually pretty meaningless if you are using it to "keep score" or to buy a bunch of stuff that really doesn't give you any sort of real happiness or fulfillment beyond that fleeting excitement of purchasing something shiny and new. We've all heard the stories of lottery winners who lose not only all their money, but also everything they cared about in the process. Most thought the money and the lifestyle it afforded would change how they felt on the inside, but it actually just made them feel empty, because they used it on things that didn't really matter at the end of the day, and lost sight of who they really were and what really mattered.

It turns out we've gotten the money thing wrong for years. Money is not about consumption, or status, or some sort of score that defines how well you are doing in your life. It's not even about living the Instagram life—full of luxurious trips to glamorous destinations that make the rest of us feel like we are missing out. Even that feels empty after the novelty wears off.

Instead, money is about freedom. Freedom from stress. Freedom to discover who you want to become, what you want to do with your talents and time that will truly make you feel happy, excited, and fulfilled. Freedom to be able to live the life that gives you that deep, enduring sense of fulfillment knowing you are happy with who you are, what you are doing, how you are living, and, most importantly, the impact you are making.

Here's the crazy thing that almost no one would expect looking at my life now: My money story isn't defined by getting drafted (though that was an absolute godsend financially). Instead, it is defined by the education and guidance I got and chose to follow—the very same education and guidance that is in this book. The reason I am where I am today is because I got introduced to Financial Finesse early in my life after college (all players have access to Financial Finesse's coaching program as a benefit provided by the NFL Players Association), and instead of falling into the very easy temptation of spending all my football earnings (something very easy to do when you are so used to scrambling to get by), I chose to follow the guidance outlined in Financial Finesse's START™ framework—the same framework you'll go through in this book. The principles in this simple framework shifted my entire perspective on money and the way I used it to truly achieve a much happier, more fulfilling life.

As I went through this process you are about to go through in this book, everything became clearer. I saved most of my money from football, and now am able to focus on my true purpose—charitable giving and volunteering—which I've turned into a business of my own by starting an app called Rayze to connect people with charitable causes that match their interests and passions.

I promise you, even though your story is likely very different from mine, if you follow the START™ framework outlined in this book, it will lead to things you never thought possible.

Your purpose awaits.

Carl Nassib, NFL player and Fintech Entrepreneur

INTRODUCTION

"MONEY MONEY MONEY MONEY! MONEY!"

"For the Love of Money" by the O'Jays hit number 3 on the US Billboard R&B chart through its clever repetition of one of the most powerful words in the English language—a word that, in one way or another, evokes a visceral response in all of us: "money."

When we think of the song, many of us may connect it to TV shows and movies where it's been used to glorify a life of luxury. But the reality is actually much different. In between the "Money money money money! MONEY!" chorus, the song gets really dark, with chilling lyrics about what people will do for money—lyrics that cite "stealing from their mother" and "robbing their brother" among even more desperate, soul-crushing acts that don't belong in a personal finance book. Perhaps the most insightful lyric is "for a small piece of paper, it carries a lot of weight" (keeping in mind the word "weight" here is an understatement considering the desperate level of poverty faced by Blacks and other marginalized groups in the post-Civil Rights era in which the song was written). Granted, the song was written back when people regularly used cash—as opposed to the world we live in now where credit cards and electronic payments are much more the norm. But the sentiment still applies—money, in whatever form we use it, carries a lot of weight.

Having run a financial coaching company for the last 23 years, I have seen firsthand the deep-seated emotions people experience when our coaches talk to them about money. Money—both the word and the concept—almost inevitably triggers immediate reactions in people, bringing forth a very complex, love-hate relationship that, to quote the O'Jays, "can drive some people out of their minds."

Aspirationally, having a lot of money evokes childhood dreams of a life of luxury that we are almost all programmed to covet—a life we imagine to be not only stress-free, but deeply exciting and glamorous, where we can afford the best of everything—the clothes, the cars, the jewelry, the houses, the private air travel to luxurious locations and all the five-star perks that come with that. This is why the lottery is so popular and people go into a frenzy when there's a huge jackpot. Money is the ultimate fantasy, and even in our darkest hours, we never completely lose that fantasy—that feeling of what it would be like to be incredibly wealthy with a seemingly unlimited ability to buy anything we want any time we want and never have to worry about the consequences.

On the other side of the equation, money, at its most basic level, represents self-preservation, because it is a resource we need to live and provide for our families. We need money for our safety and survival. Consider those facing life threatening illnesses requiring expensive treatments or people forced to stay in abusive relationships because they don't have enough money to leave their spouse or partner. In these circumstances, money is quite literally the difference between life and death. Our human brains process this and unconsciously consider the lack of money a threat to our very existence—releasing the same "fight-or-flight" hormones that come when we are confronted with a life-or-death situation.

And because of this dynamic, the mere mention of money is stressful for most people. It is something most of us feel we don't ever seem to have enough of; it's a word that automatically triggers a sense of scarcity and deep inadequacy, because we know how vital it is to our lives and yet don't ever feel like we have it under control. Will we have enough to pay the bills? Will we have enough to provide the life we want for ourselves and our families? Why does it feel like everyone else seems to have more money than we do, or an easier time managing it? Why can't we seem to ever get ahead? When will we finally be free of having it dictate the choices we make in life, of having it consume our thoughts on a near-constant basis?

The reality is that money can be a prison that holds us captive to doing whatever is necessary to stay afloat, or it can be one of the greatest sources of freedom that fuels our ability to live an incredibly meaningful, fulfilling, purposeful life. And that is the reason I've decided to write this book. Our relationship with money doesn't need to be fraught with anxiety, desperation, or despair. We've worked with millions of people, from all walks of life, to transform their financial lives so they can live life on their own terms—so they no longer are burdened with financial stress, no longer have to make choices that compromise their integrity, self-esteem, or happiness. We've worked with people who have gone from hundreds of thousands of dollars of debt to full financial security. We've worked with people who were a day or two away from eviction and helped them turn their lives around so they ultimately became homeowners or even landlords themselves!

THE LIFE-CHANGING MAGIC OF TIDYING UP YOUR FINANCES

When you change the way you think about and manage your money, your entire life changes for the better. You don't have to stay in a toxic or abusive relationship for financial reasons; you don't need to work at a job you hate; you don't need to make compromises around your children's education or limit the opportunities you provide them. When you gain control over your finances, you can ultimately spend your time doing what provides you with the most joy and fulfillment and make what Steve Jobs called "your own dent in the universe."

And that is really the true power of money: It gives you choices you would otherwise never have. It gives you the opportunity to achieve what famed psychologist Abraham Maslow called "self-actualization"—reaching a place where how you live your life is fully aligned with your greatest talents, values, passions, and beliefs. Money, used to facilitate this kind of personal growth, is fuel to create a "life well lived"—a life you can look back on with pride, knowing that you did what was right for you, your family, your community; that you made an impact and you created a legacy that will endure long after you are gone.

I realize that this sounds ridiculously aspirational. In the United States, 65 percent of employed Americans are financially struggling, and an additional 4 percent are in a state of financial crisis where they are close to being or are homeless and facing food insecurity. That's nearly 70 percent of the adult working population in what is supposed to be one of the wealthiest nations in the world!

Even those lucky enough to not be struggling are often still under financial pressures and stress that impact their quality of life. Of the 31 percent of Americans that have reached financial stability—meaning they are making ends meet and making progress toward key financial goals—over two-thirds report that they are financially stressed.

So how do you go from wherever you are financially—which likely includes at least some stress and anxiety—to a place where you have enough money to live life on your own terms, free of the money worries you carry around with you every day?

It's definitely a process, but the good news is that we've helped millions of people accomplish this transformation over the last 23 years. And while they all have unique stories and journeys, they have five keys to success in common that anyone can employ. We call it the START™ framework:

Set Yourself up for Financial Success
Tackle Your Financial Stress
Advance Toward the Life You Want
Role Model Good Financial Habits and Behaviors
Thrive by Living Your Purpose

This book will take you through each step so you can create a plan to build the life you want—the life of purpose, impact, and incredible fulfillment where you don't have to worry about money, aren't chained to other people's expectations, aren't forced to make tough choices that compromise your joy or integrity, and can afford to do what you believe you were put on this earth to do.

HOW I DISCOVERED THE POWER OF THE START™ FRAMEWORK

Before we get into the START™ framework, I want to address the elephant in the room. I imagine you, the reader, are thinking, "Who is this woman, and what proof does she have that this START™ framework truly works when pretty much everything else I've tried to improve my finances has ultimately failed?"

Well, it's a long story, but I'll start with today and work backward.

Today I'm the founder and CEO of Financial Finesse, the nation's leading provider of financial wellness coaching, delivered as an employee benefit, to millions of employees at over 12,000 organizations across the country.

We use the START™ framework to help people from all walks of life to achieve financial independence, from minimum wage employees to CEOs, from employees facing serious financial crises, to those who simply can't seem to get ahead, to those who are terrified of losing the wealth they have built and are held hostage by that terror. But the START™ framework described in this book wasn't created overnight. It took years of working with millions of employees to develop. And it took the right circumstances—including starting a company whose entire mission and business model was dependent on helping people change their financial lives, rather than on selling financial products, services, and investments, which often ended up benefiting financial representatives at the expense of the customers they served.

I started the company way back in 1999, after running an investment management firm catering to high-net-worth investors and discovering that they had major holes in their financial plans, putting themselves at risk for losing a large percentage of the money most had worked so hard to build. I began to realize that we had a whole industry (myself included at that time) focused on selling financial products, services, investments, and advice, but virtually no one out there was dedicated to truly helping people make the best decisions without a sales pitch attached, especially for those who needed it most.

So I looked around. I searched for organizations whose sole mission and focus was to educate people about their finances, on a personal level, in a way that could impact their financial decision-making for the better and ultimately change their financial lives. Obviously, there were plenty of financial advisors—hundreds of thousands in fact—and almost as many financial products, services, and securities. But the system was broken. Back then, if you were in the financial business, your livelihood depended on commissions from selling financial products or services. Unfortunately, this was a complete departure from what so many people actually needed—which was ongoing personalized guidance on how they could improve their personal financial situation, from someone they could trust implicitly to prioritize their financial needs without the conflict of interest that comes from making a living selling commission-based financial products and services. The vast majority of people needed someone who could help them with all aspects of their finances—from reducing debt, to improving credit, to saving to achieve their most important life goals—so they could set themselves up for success instead of putting themselves at risk.

As I went through this process and discovered that this service *did not* exist, I began to peel back the onion and find out why such a needed service wasn't available. What I found was horrifying: Financial coaching didn't exist because the financial services industry had such an incredibly strong foothold that people were inadvertently brainwashed to think that the only way they could improve their finances was to go to a financial services representative (or broker) who would then sell them financial products and services, with the hope that their broker somehow had the ability to see into the future and invest their money in whatever would give them the highest return. While the financial services industry has come a long way since then, there wasn't even an acknowledgment at that time that the vast majority of Americans didn't have enough money to qualify for this "service," which typically required minimum investments beyond what they could afford. So that was also a big miss that no one was talking about—that the trillion-dollar financial services industry was completely ignoring those most in need of financial help—hardworking people who didn't have a fortune to manage, but needed help figuring out how to pay down debt, make ends meet, and over time, achieve important financial goals for themselves and their families. No one was focused on this segment of the market, at least in a way that would permanently change people's financial lives for the better.

When I realized this, I decided that I *had* to start a company to address this issue or I would regret it for the rest of my life. I left the money management industry for good, and embarked on what would become the greatest, most rewarding, crazy, beautiful, challenging adventure of my life: starting Financial Finesse.

Back then, it seemed like the best way to help people who needed completely unbiased financial guidance was to go directly to them, through workshops designed to show people how they could manage their compensation and benefits to achieve their goals—and without taking undue risk, which was the norm at the time. And in Los Angeles and San Francisco, where I had large personal networks, things took off, and we got not only a steady stream of attendees but people asking for additional classes so they could learn more. Outside of Los Angeles and San Francisco, however, it simply wasn't a sustainable business model, because we had such significant marketing costs. It became obvious the company would run out of money if we didn't do something.

Fortunately, as I've discovered often happens in life and in business, an opportunity I never anticipated emerged and literally saved our company. One day after a Financial Finesse workshop in San Francisco, a woman approached me and asked what I would charge to do a series of workshops at her company, for her employees. I still remember the room, where I was standing, the look of anticipation on her face as she wondered if I was going to come up with a reasonable fee or not. I blurted out "$500 a workshop!" thinking that was a whole lot of money without any marketing costs to get people to attend but still reasonable for a large corporation. Well, it turned out it was more than reasonable. She thanked me, she gave me her card and a big hug, and we finalized all the details that week. And as they say, the rest is history. If this moment hadn't come, I don't think I'd be writing this book today and certainly wouldn't have been able to create an organization that has worked with millions of employees to change their financial lives. Today over 12,000 employers offer our financial coaching as an employer paid benefit—available to all employees, on an unlimited basis, free of charge.

If you look at where we started and where we are today, it sounds like this amazing success story, but keep in mind, we are 23 years into this journey of providing completely unbiased financial coaching. Calling our company a success story is a massive oversimplification of all the challenges we faced, literally going head-to-head against a trillion-dollar financial services industry that, I came to find out, didn't want people to have the financial education we were providing. Back when I started Financial Finesse, most financial services representatives were trained to make finances seem so incredibly complex that potential customers would throw up their hands in frustration and relent to using a financial services representative to handle what felt overwhelming to do themselves. We literally had threats from multiple financial services companies that they would "spend us out of business" doing "the same" financial education for free that companies paid us to deliver.

Fortunately, the employers who hired us to provide unbiased financial education to their employees were very progressive in their thinking and saw those tactics for what they were—opportunities for financial services firms to use their employees as a sales channel. But those employers were still very much the minority at that time—few and far between in a world that didn't yet see the implications of financial services salespeople on the worksite, selling in the guise of educating.

At the time, it cost me a lot of sleepless nights, but looking back I now see it as one of the best things that ever happened to our company, for one simple reason: We had no choice but to be incredibly effective in what we did, or else we simply wouldn't be able to keep and grow our client base and ultimately survive as a business.

This meant hiring the best and brightest CERTIFIED FINANCIAL PLANNER™ professionals to be financial coaches for the vast majority of people who weren't getting any real financial help. It also meant changing our model from giving workshops only, which can inspire and impact people over the short term, to providing real financial wellness coaching where our coaches work side by side with employees to help them progress financially and achieve their most important life goals. And it meant getting employers to see that this was a true benefit—that when employees work with a coach to make the best use of not only their compensation but also their employee benefits, the employers win as well by having happier, healthier, more engaged, loyal, and productive employees who aren't tempted to leave for pennies on the dollar in an effort to improve their finances.

Fast-forward to today, and financial coaching is a growing industry. More employers are offering it, the right way, from companies like ours that don't sell financial products and services but instead provide coaching as an employer-paid benefit. It's wonderful to see all the progress that has been made and all the lives that have been impacted. For that reason, I will always be an advocate for financial coaching—whether from our firm or any other firm—as long as the sole mission and business model centers on helping people improve their finances.

But I'm also an advocate for those who don't have this kind of benefit at work, and who can't afford to pay for it, and that's why I chose to write this book. It's my best attempt to offer everything that has proved to be incredibly effective in helping people change their financial lives by using the START™ framework I shared above—a framework that people in any financial situation can use—to make both immediate and lifelong improvements to their finances. So even if you don't have a financial coaching benefit at work or aren't yet ready to use it, you have something you can use to get from where you are today to where you want to be, and to create the most fulfilling life possible in the process.

Now, with no further ado, let's get STARTed!

1

GETTING STARTed

AN INTRODUCTION TO
THE FIVE MODULES IN
THE START™ FRAMEWORK

The START™ framework is designed to be imminently flexible, a program you can work throughout your life, regardless of where you are financially. It's also something you may want to revisit regularly in part or in whole to adapt as your life evolves and adapts.

All that said, if you are in serious financial stress—in a position where you are in danger of losing your home or having trouble providing yourself and your family with basic necessities, please skip directly to Chapter 9, which will give you tips on how to get back on your feet. Then, once you have some breathing room, come back to this section and go through the framework.

If you are not in a financial crisis, it's best to start at the beginning and go through the framework in the order intended, with the understanding that you will want to focus most on the sections that are most relevant to where you are today.

NOTE

This book is designed to help people across the entire financial spectrum. This book is for you whether you are struggling financially, are trying to plan for the future balancing multiple priorities in a time of significant economic and market uncertainty, or are financially independent but want to make sure you stay that way. There's a lot covered here that may not be relevant to you today but will be in the future. You'll get the most value out of it if you focus on the areas that will help you now, which will mean skipping anything that isn't relevant to your current situation. However, it's equally important to understand that your finances will change over time, and part of committing to this framework means actively revisiting it a least once a year to make sure that you are on track. I also recommend revisiting this framework whenever you go through major life changes that impact your finances—going to the sections most relevant to you to figure out how to best navigate those changes.

Here's a breakdown of each part of the START™ framework. There are five key modules:

Set Yourself up for Financial Success

Tackle Your Financial Stress

Advance Toward the Life You Want

Role Model Good Financial Habits and Behaviors

Thrive by Living Your Purpose

I've included brief descriptions of each module below to give you a sense of what to expect before we delve into each in depth. Along with the descriptions, you'll find reflection questions you can use to prepare for each module so you can make the most of each based on your financial situation and life goals.

MODULE 1: SET YOURSELF UP FOR FINANCIAL SUCCESS

The first module is all about building a solid foundation that will set you up for financial success. This may be a bit counterintuitive. Conventional wisdom would dictate that when you want to make progress, you need to start with your goals and work backward. The problem with that approach is that without a solid foundation set up to foster the financial habits and behaviors needed to ultimately achieve your goals, you are likely to run into the same financial challenges again and again, and this can seriously hinder your ability not only to meet your financial goals in the first place, but to sustain and build upon them. That's why this first module is all about what you can do to build that foundation. It dramatically increases your odds of success by leveraging the most powerful resource you have—you!

When you look at what drives sustainable financial security, where money is no longer an object in the decisions you make because you have enough to live the life you want, it's actually not how much people make, or the way they invest, that drives the majority of their success. These things are important and have the potential to accelerate or derail your progress, but what matters most is not the major life decisions, but the culmination of all the minor ones—the way you manage your money day in and day out.

Most people aren't all that intentional about this, and as a result, they end up behind where they want to be financially, feeling that they are "treading water" versus making meaningful progress. Worse, this is all happening despite enormous amounts of effort on their part. Most people are trying very hard to overcome this dynamic, forcing themselves to summon all their willpower to avoid overspending; fighting with their spouses over money in an effort to get their partners on board with the way they feel money should be borrowed, spent, saved, or invested; obsessively checking their investments with the thought that more oversight somehow means better results . . . And the list goes on and on and on.

This module gives you the keys to unlock what really drives long-term financial success so that you can get much farther, much faster, and actually have fun in the process. You'll learn about the power of money scripts—the subconscious beliefs that are likely sabotaging you without your even realizing it—and how to rewrite your own money script to support your financial success. You'll learn how to form a financial identity, building upon your existing values, so that you can predecide how to manage your money in line with your identity, without having to rely on tapping into your willpower, which, as we'll discuss in further chapters, is a recipe for failure. Last, you'll learn how to accelerate the financial progress you make from your new money script and financial identity by examining the key factors, or "bright spots," that have driven your greatest accomplishments so you can apply those same practices to your finances and develop the habits, routines, and environment you need to finalize the process of setting yourself up for success.

This will require some up-front work, but once you have these techniques ingrained into your daily life, you'll be able to supercharge your financial progress without all the wasted effort, the money fights, and the shame and sheer exhaustion that come from feeling you can't seem to get to where you want to be financially. And you'll have the financial foundation in place to move through the rest of the steps in the framework with relative ease.

Reflection Questions to Prepare for Module 1: Set Yourself up for Financial Success

How do you currently make spending, borrowing, saving, or investing decisions? What is working, and what is counterproductive, requiring too much effort for little or no result and exhausting you in the process?

When have you accomplished something you are proud of, where you had to overcome obstacles to get to a successful result? Write down as many examples as you can think of, along with the things you did with each that drove your success. Examples can be as big or small as you like—from overcoming a learning disability, to improving your marriage, to getting to finally cleaning the basement, to figuring out a way to get your hard-to-wrangle child to class on time. The important thing is to focus on accomplishments that didn't come easy for you initially, where you prevailed despite the challenges you faced.

MODULE 2: TACKLE YOUR FINANCIAL STRESS

After you've set yourself up for financial success, you'll have a strong foundation to build upon to take the next step, which is to tackle your financial stress. This step is second because the momentum from the first module will make it much easier to reduce your stress and will ensure that you have the structure in place to continually improve your finances so you can overcome the financial challenges that are causing your financial stress in the first place.

Also, stress reduction in and of itself is hugely important to your long-term financial success, because financial stress is expensive and can become a constant drain on your finances if you don't address it. Here's why:

1. It causes direct expenses, because stress takes a serious toll on both your mental and physical health and not only increases your healthcare expenses but causes short- and long-term disabilities that compromise your ability to perform at work (or in some cases to work at all). According to an AP-AOL Health Poll, people with high financial stress are over 3 times more likely than those with low financial stress to have ulcers or digestive track issues, 3 times more likely to have migraines or other headaches, 6 times more likely to suffer from depression, and 2 times more likely to have a heart attack (see Figure 1.1)—and this is just part of a long list of both chronic and life-threatening conditions that are correlated with financial stress.[1]

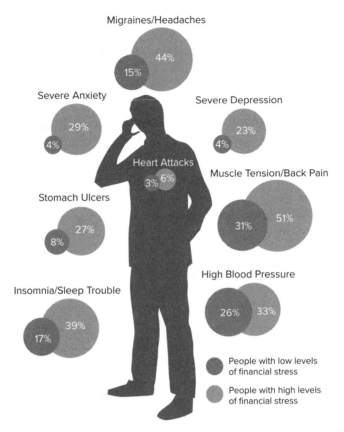

FIGURE 1.1 Stress takes a serious toll on both your mental and physical health.

And as you might imagine, those under financial stress end up spending significantly more on healthcare expenses, which in turn worsens their financial situation and further increases their financial stress. The good news is that with the right support (including the tips outlined in this chapter), you can reverse the mental, physical, and financial costs of financial stress. A study conducted by Financial Finesse found that healthcare expenses for employees who engaged in financial coaching to reduce their financial stress fell 4.5 percent, while healthcare expenses for employees who did not engage in financial coaching to address their financial stress rose more than 19 percent.

2. Improving your sense of well-being enables you to be the best version of yourself and gives you the clarity of mind to make the better decisions and focus on the areas of your life that support your long-term financial security—from the quality of your relationships to your productivity and performance at work. In its 2022 report "Helping Employees Manage Debt," the Financial Health Network found that 50 percent of respondents who reported that debt is a source of stress for them said that they had spent on average at least one hour per week at work dealing with debt-related issues (e.g., contacting creditors) in the past month, and 29 percent report that debt stress has impacted their work performance.[2]

This module is designed to help you break the cycle of financial stress, regardless of whether your stress is from serious financial challenges, frustrations that you are not able to get ahead and achieve key goals, or a sense of impending doom that the economy or stock market will cause you to lose the savings you've worked so hard to build.

You'll learn to reduce your financial stress through a three-step process: First, you'll examine how you feel about your finances, how and why those feelings are causing you stress, and how you can best manage that stress, understanding it may take time to improve the financial circumstances that are causing it. Second, you'll identify the root cause of your financial stress so you can move toward improving your finances in the areas causing you the most stress. (One chapter in particular, Chapter 7, is devoted to showing you how to navigate difficult life events that have upended your finances.) Third, you'll put together a plan to bulletproof your finances against future financial stress so you can sleep comfortably at night, knowing you are well protected against any financial challenge life throws your way.

NOTE

The last chapter in this module—Chapter 9—is specifically designed for those in financial crisis. If this is your situation, *go immediately to Chapter 9.*

Reflection Questions to Prepare for Module 2: Tackle Your Financial Stress

How high is your financial stress right now? Rate yourself on a scale from 1 to 5, where 1 means having little to no ongoing financial stress, with only occasional spikes in stress when you face a specific financial challenge, and 5 means being so preoccupied you are physically ailing, not sleeping or eating, etc.

If you could change three things about your finances to reduce your stress, what would they be? Examples here include things like earning more income, paying off debt, or determining how to make the best financial decisions about navigating challenging life events, such as getting through a divorce, death of a spouse, or disability that has rendered you unable to work.

What are the best ways that you've found to manage your stress, and how can you put together a self-care plan based on that? Have you found midafternoon walks help? A therapist or friend to talk to? Or intentionally engaging with professionals to empower you to find effective tools to change your circumstances?

MODULE 3: ADVANCE TOWARD THE LIFE YOU WANT

Unlike the first two modules, which are all about building an incredibly strong financial foundation, this module focuses on your financial future. In this module, you'll learn what you need to do to create the life you want for yourself and your loved ones, while still preserving—and ideally improving—your current quality of life.

This module takes a different approach to traditional financial planning, which focuses on setting and planning for key financial goals. While traditional planning is a critical part of the process of creating the life you want to live, it falls short for many people, who struggle to find a way to effectively balance their current needs with future goals or end up achieving their goals, only to discover afterward that they don't actually align with the life they want to live.

In this module you'll learn how to dramatically improve your odds of achieving the financial goals that are integral to building the life you want. To do this, you will need to take a step back from traditional financial planning and really envision the life you want based on what will drive the greatest sense of happiness and fulfillment for you, including what you need to do to take proper care of yourself so you don't wind up sacrificing your current needs in an effort to attain future goals. When you integrate these key areas into the planning process, you not only achieve your individual financial goals, but live a much more meaningful life in the process.

As you go through this module, you'll create a vision of your ideal life based on your most important values—a life filled with meaning, fulfillment, and joy—and work backward to determine how to identify, prioritize, and plan for key financial goals that are integral to building the life you want.

By the end of this module, you'll walk away with a step-by-step plan you can start to put in place immediately to begin building the future you always wanted, but may never have thought was actually possible.

Reflection Questions for Module 3: Advance Toward the Life You Want

What matters most to you in life? Here are some questions to help you define your vision of an incredibly satisfying, meaningful life:

Do you want a life partner, and if so, do you want to get married, have a domestic partnership, or simply enjoy a long-term committed relationship? Or are you happiest without this level of commitment, which means taking care of your finances on your own?

Do you want children, or do you want a life where you can do what you want when you want (for any of you who have yet to embark on the journey that is parenthood, this is the opposite of life with children)?

Are you a nester who needs to have a home that makes you feel safe and provides that sense of stability and comfort that many of us need to stay grounded? Or are you more nomadic, an adventurer who loves to live somewhere for a couple of years and then move for a change of pace and a chance to experience a new culture?

What are other key life milestones that you feel are integral to building the life you want?

MODULE 4: ROLE MODEL GOOD FINANCIAL HABITS AND BEHAVIORS

This module fills another major gap in the current thinking about financial wellness. Too often, financial coaching operates in a silo, and financial coaches work solely with individuals on their personal challenges and goals. The reality, however, is that life includes so many other factors—partners and spouses, children, extended family, and even friends—all who influence and are influenced by our financial wellness. And most coaching never contemplates the impact that one individual can have on the larger community, especially future generations who, without the right role models, are likely to face downward financial mobility.

We, as humans, are social creatures who are programmed to imitate the attitudes, actions, and behaviors of those closest to us or those we consciously choose to emulate, like mentors or role models. Remember those statistics from the Introduction—65 percent of employed Americans are financially struggling, and 4 percent more are in a state of financial crisis? We can't begin to change those statistics without approaching financial wellness as a movement larger than ourselves.

If you are like most people my staff and I work with, as you progress financially, you'll naturally want to spread the word and become a role model for others, and you'll find it incredibly fulfilling to do so. This doesn't mean you have to share every detail of your financial journey; it doesn't even mean that you have to go public at all. If you are incredibly private, you can still "pay it forward" just by living the principles you adopt. Trust me; your friends, family, coworkers, and, most importantly, your children will take notice. We tend to follow people's actions more than their words, so simply putting what you learn from this book into practice can have an incredible impact on others.

But beyond the impact you can have on others, there's a potentially bigger reason to actively role model good financial habits and behaviors, and that's the impact it has on you. When you see your actions as having implications far beyond the effect on your own life, you will be in a position where you feel a sense of accountability to those who follow your lead. When times get hard, you'll have another reason to stay the course—knowing that others are watching and are looking to you for inspiration. With the responsibility of behaving in ways you want another to emulate comes the possibility of self-improvement, growth, and increased insight.

The results of a study of 200 male and female patients demonstrate the power of being a role model. The patients were selected at random from all patients admitted to an inpatient alcohol treatment facility and were surveyed 10 years following treatment that included participation in Alcoholics Anonymous (AA).[3] The study found that respondents whose involvement in AA included continued sponsorship of other members throughout the follow-up period were 50 percent more likely to be in complete or stable remission (91 percent versus 61 percent for all respondents).

Being a sponsor increases self-awareness, social skills, and social competence when it comes to engaging with others. In addition, sponsors derive an increased sense of psychological wellbeing and positive social approval from helping others. Over the longer term, sponsorship can become a meaningful and purposeful activity, as it allows those providing it to be productive, find meaning, and maintain a non-addicted identity. Additionally, sponsorship is a process that is beneficial for those who have little access to wider social networks.

Changing habits to become healthier, whether financially, physically, spiritually, or mentally, is difficult, because we tend to gravitate toward those things that provide us with instant gratification versus doing the harder work needed to build the lives we want. If you follow the START™ framework, you will be replacing old financial habits and behaviors with better ones and creating a whole new financial identity. That's not easy work, and even as your new habits and identity become ingrained in the way you live your life, you will face challenges and setbacks that increase the temptation to revert to what feels good in the moment. That's the nature of being human. Role modeling is one of the most effective tools to counteract this—and to do so in a way that can change others' lives for the better.

Reflection Questions for Module 4:
Role Model Good Financial Habits and Behaviors

Who have been your greatest positive role models? These people can be anyone from parents, to teachers, to mentors, or even bosses, coworkers, and friends whom you admire and have learned important life lessons from. You can include people who simply led by example without intentionally imparting their wisdom, or those who took the time to teach you critical life skills that benefit you to this day.

How is your life better as a result of knowing them and learning from them? What did they model for you or teach you that has influenced you to develop positive behaviors and habits and make good life decisions? Examples include learning personal discipline, like being organized or on time; learning how to manage relationships; learning how to cope with stress; and developing important habits that support your physical, financial, or mental health.

What hard financial challenges have you had to deal with that you'd love to help others avoid? Examples include getting into debt; not having enough money saved for an emergency; wasting money on things that you didn't get enjoyment out of and losing the chance to invest that money instead; or picking the wrong health insurance plan or not considering insurance at all and having to struggle financially after a life-altering event as a result. *Bottom line:* Almost all of us have financial lessons that we've learned the hard way—lessons that we'd love to impart to others so they don't have to experience the same challenges.

If you have children, what is your vision for how they will manage their finances as adults?

MODULE 5: THRIVE BY LIVING YOUR PURPOSE

The final module, which is all about living your purpose, is an incredibly compelling concept. We all seek meaning in life, and we get a deep level of emotional fulfillment that comes from knowing that we made an impact—that all the crazy obstacles, challenges, and traumas we faced were well worth it because they shaped a legacy that will live long after we do.

Deep, I know. I've thought about this . . . a few thousand/million times. . . .

But in all that thinking, it still feels so . . . incredibly aspirational. . . . Even as you progress toward having the flexibility to live your purpose, there are countless moments of self-doubt—so many times you question whether you are actually making progress, so many times when it takes most of your energy to get out of bed in the morning and face the day. There are times you will feel hopeless, like you are never going to get to where you want to be; and even when you do reach a state of financial independence, there are plenty of times you question whether you are making the most of it. It's aspirational both to think that you can get to a place where money is no longer a reason for the major life choices you make and to think that somehow when you reach financial security, your purpose will just magically appear.

I'm right there with you. When I didn't have money or access to it, it was nearly impossible to imagine what life would be like not having to worry about it. At that point, even thinking about a "purpose" felt abstract. And now that I do have enough money to not have to worry, I still have moments of doubt. With this company I run and the work we do to change financial lives, with the people I employ who have become like family to me, with my son whom I love more than I imagined was possible and a loving and supportive husband, I know and often feel that I am blessed beyond belief. I do genuinely believe on my best days that I'm doing what I was put on this earth to do—living the life I was meant to live. But then there's a lot of time in between those moments of clarity where I get caught up in the challenges of life and wonder if I'm on the right track.

I'm here to tell you that your feelings are *normal*. Living your purpose is not a state of nirvana. It is more of a feeling of having a North Star that's guiding you—a feeling that when everything is going to hell, there's meaning to what you are doing, how you are living, what you are learning, and whom you are teaching. It's being able to have the financial freedom to do your best, whatever that means to you, and knowing you have the freedom to continue to evolve and grow and figure it all out.

And that, in that process, you don't have to make decisions or choices because of financial pressures or concerns and can instead focus on what you feel really matters, where you think you can make the biggest impact.

Bottom line: Living a purposeful life is still living life . . . with all the ups and downs that come with it.

No one, not even the wealthiest among us, has infinite financial resources, and certainly none of us has infinite wisdom. Life is about progressing, losing your footing, getting back up, and moving forward again. The closer you are to full financial security, the more you can remove money as a variable you have to consider in the choices you make. The gift of not having to worry about money gives you more room to pursue the things you care most about, and that's the essence of this last module—having that freedom to figure out what is truly the best use of your time and talents, how you create meaning out of this crazy journey called life.

I can't give you answers here and won't even try. But I can help you free yourself from the financial constraints that hold you back, so you can begin finding your own answers. That's the purpose of this last module, to show you what is possible at different levels of financial security, and to prompt you to begin thinking about what you would do if money wasn't an object, because if you follow all the previous modules, you'll get to a point where it truly isn't. And trust me, you'll want to be prepared when you do.

Module 1

SET YOURSELF UP FOR FINANCIAL SUCCESS

ABOUT THIS MODULE

If you regularly read personal finance books or follow personal finance gurus, you know that virtually all the focus is on financial tips you can take to improve your finances. And there's nothing wrong with that. The content is generally correct from a financial planning perspective. It usually centers on ways to spend less, save more, pay down debt, improve your credit, invest prudently, reduce your tax bill, protect yourself from losing money, and avoid financial mistakes. The problem is, similar to what we see when it comes to creating a healthy lifestyle, it's so much easier said than done. When it comes to health, we all know it's important to follow a balanced, healthy diet, exercise regularly, and get that eight hours of sleep we are told is so vital. Knowledge is not the problem. Changing our behavior is. Unless you are like my niece who was born with a taste for vegetables as opposed to the more savory, sugar-laden foods most of us find so compelling, it's one thing to know you shouldn't eat doughnuts for breakfast but a whole other thing entirely to replace those doughnuts with some sort of healthy green juice concoction.

Same thing with finances. We know we need to live within our means, to manage our debt and credit "responsibly," to avoid making impulsive or emotional investment decisions. We know that it's better to actually plan for taxes (especially as our income grows or if we are doing work as an independent contractor) instead of scrambling at the last minute to simply file them on time. We know that having insurance and having a will or trust are important, but it's far too easy to procrastinate because we don't want to go through what is a time-consuming and often emotionally difficult process of thinking how to protect ourselves from the bad things that could happen to us and our families. So we hear the experts, and we may even follow the tips for a little while, but then life happens, and our innate human nature inevitably intervenes and derails us.

I want to state something very important here. *This is not just normal; it's innately human.* It's deeply embedded in our brain chemistry to do things that feel good at the expense of things that are best for us long term. Brain researchers have discovered that the area of the brain that exercises will-power and forgoes immediate gratification to make good long-term choices is both the smallest and the least powerful part of the brain. It does exist, and we can and do tap it when we have a plethora of energy, but it tires very quickly if we force ourselves to make too many decisions that delay our short-term gratification in favor of our long-term best interest. The idea that people fail at a diet or exercise regimen, or that they spend more money than they have despite having a budget in place, because they don't have enough character or willpower is not just blatantly wrong, but dangerous. Why? Because "gutting it out" is not a sustainable way to make good deci-sions. Some may be able to hang on a little longer than others, but even that doesn't help them in the end, because they tend to backslide in a bigger way. And let's face it: That constant tension between doing what you really want to do and doing what you are "supposed to do" can be incredibly stressful because you are constantly fighting temptation and feeling either deprived if you win the fight or ashamed if you lose.

The best thing you can do, right here, right now, is to stop this insan-ity and accept that, for better or worse, just like the other 8 billion people on earth, you are human and subject to all the challenges that come with that. You can't overcome your own humanity by trying harder to do the "right things." But you can work with both your human nature and your individual personality to set yourself up for success by flipping the script on your brain and removing willpower from the equation altogether, so that it is fun, easy, and automatic to make financial decisions that are in your best interest. You can literally get yourself to a point where it's automatic to make the best financial decisions for your life, where not doing so actually causes extreme psychological discomfort.

This module provides you with a three-step process to do just that and to free up your money and sanity in the process: (1) identifying and refining your money script, (2) establishing your financial identity, and (3) figuring out how to identify what drives your personal success—what researchers call your bright spots—so you can apply those same techniques to accelerate your financial process. It's time to stop punishing yourself and instead set yourself up to succeed without relying on the very limited supply of willpower the brain is able to muster. Read on to learn how.

2

IDENTIFY AND REVISE YOUR MONEY SCRIPT

The first step in setting yourself up for financial success goes back to a concept introduced in the previous chapter—which is to determine what your money script actually is—that subconscious set of attitudes, beliefs, values, and experiences that has shaped the way you view and manage your money and influenced virtually all your financial decisions. Up until now, your money script has likely been running in the background, guiding your relationship with money without your even realizing it, but it doesn't have to be that way. If you pay attention to how you respond to different financial situations, you'll discover that money scripts are part of the story we tell ourselves—and come through in the form of self-talk as we go throughout our days. Do any of these sound like you?

- When you open your credit card statement and see your total balance, do you feel a sense of shame, that somehow having debt means you are bad at money? Do you take that a step further and feel that you will never be able to pay off all your debt, that it's a permanently hopeless situation, because people like you don't ever get good opportunities in life? Do you view it as a setback that you are determined to overcome, and become more motivated to figure out how to get out of debt as soon as possible? Or do you accept it as the reality you are in currently, without judging yourself, and assume that with time you will earn more money and be able to pay off the debt—in other words, do you believe the situation will take care of itself because in your experience, it always does?

■ When your account balance in your 401(k) goes down, what is the first thing you tell yourself? Do you immediately personalize it and think of it as further proof you are "bad" at investing? Do you catastrophize and jump to obsessing over your retirement being in jeopardy? Do you panic and sell off all your investments in an effort to protect yourself from further losses because you've learned you have to be very careful not to ever lose money? Do you see it as a buying opportunity because "buy low, sell high" is ingrained in your money script? Or do you simply process it as a temporary event and move on?

■ When you are with friends who spend a lot more money on a meal than you can comfortably afford, do you feel inferior, ashamed, like you somehow are behind in life? Do you think of them as foolish for overspending, knowing they likely don't really have the money to pay for the meal? Or do you simply take note and decide that you are going to have to be careful about how often you dine out with them for the sake of your own finances?

By examining how you respond to these and the myriad of other situations you face on a near daily basis regarding money, you'll find themes that define your money script, which include both negative and positive attitudes toward money and, in some cases, the best way to use it. You may uncover feelings of inadequacy and hopelessness—that you are "bad" at money and will never be able to improve your financial situation. Or on the other end of the spectrum, you may discover that you have a significant amount of financial complacency and denial—that things will be OK because they always have been. You may discover that you are incredibly hard on yourself for what you perceive to be your financial mistakes, or you may find that you process setbacks as an opportunity to learn and improve (which obviously is the healthier way to respond). You'll also discover important nuances in how you view money, such as whether you are more focused on not losing money than building wealth, or whether you are opportunistic and oriented toward finding the financial opportunity in situations, which is typically a good way to approach money, provided you don't take things too far.

As you begin to really examine your own money script, you'll start to get a clear sense of which parts of your script support your financial success and which set you up for failure. And once you do that, you'll have the clarity to change your money script for the better and retrain your subconscious to support your financial decision-making rather than derailing it. Suddenly you won't need to rely nearly as much on your brain's limited supply of willpower, because your brain will be rewired to automatically follow the new script you've set, which will support your values instead of driving your impulses.

To get you started on identifying your money script, I'm going to share my story, so you can see how this plays out in real life. This process of figuring out your money script is an incredibly vulnerable and sometimes painful process even when the story has a great ending. But once you are able to face it head-on, it not only is tremendously freeing—but will provide you with insights that help you transform how you manage your money to reduce your stress and ultimately achieve the financial freedom needed to live your purpose.

My story is a multigenerational story of financial struggle, uncertainty, and ultimately triumph. It starts with my grandparents, who passed their lessons to my parents, who eventually were able to achieve a level of financial success that their parents never could have imagined, and both directly and indirectly put me in a very privileged position that I still can't wrap my head around. It truly covers all the bases—and for much of my life was responsible for my own very complex relationship with money—much that served me but also much that didn't. You'd think as the CEO of a financial wellness company, I'd have it all together. But not so. It was only relatively recently that I went through the process of delving deep into my experiences with money and how those experiences shaped my decision-making, and how I consciously developed a new, better script.

So here goes: My parents were both the first in their families to graduate from college. Both came from relatively humble beginnings and worked their way to success. My dad got a full ride to Purdue University and another scholarship to George Washington University to pursue his legal degree. He ultimately made his way up to general counsel at Parsons Corporation after stints at the US Patent Office and a long career working in the legal department at TRW. My mom went even further academically. She achieved a PhD in American literature. For the formative years of my childhood, she was a college professor at a local community college, until she began to rankle at demands to prioritize publishing in academic journals over teaching her students in order to get tenure and decided there had to be a better way. This was the beginning of a decision that would dramatically change my life and that of my two siblings—her decision to do what I believe she was born to do—starting a business of her own and becoming one of the most successful women entrepreneurs of her time in the process.

MY DAD'S MONEY STORY

My dad came from a family of farmers in upstate New York. They labored 12 hours a day in the fields, planting, tending to, and harvesting their crops. Then they would engage in intense business negotiations to get the best possible price for what they were able to grow. But there was a paradox, as this incredibly hard work made relatively little difference in the bigger scheme of things. The weather conditions played a much bigger role in how their year would turn out than any amount of work they did, so there was this constant sense of worry—would this year be a good year, with abundance, or a really rough year, where we were barely scraping by? My Grandpa Davidson learned early the benefits of saving and frugality—because there were years he had to get his family through a poor harvest, which meant dipping into savings. Also he had to get creative. His two sons labored in the fields when they weren't at school because that saved money on workers and benefited the whole family. His wife played an active role as well, turning produce into jams and even pies to bake and sell, and feeding her own family largely off what they were able to grow that year on the farm.

The idea was to spend as little as possible, because you simply didn't know what the future would hold. To this day, I remember my Grandma Davidson coming out to visit (often for months at a time, which is another story for another book—imagine your mother-in-law buying a one-way ticket!), cooking a delicious meal with whatever we had in the refrigerator—the original "iron chef"—and then refrigerating everything left over. And by everything, I mean even a small spoonful of peas would be put in a bowl, covered with Saran wrap, and placed in the refrigerator. Of course, no one was going to eat those day-old peas—especially not us kids—but the point was that you do not ever waste food. She was socialized to think that way, and you could not convince her otherwise. I used to wonder whether the Saran wrap cost more than the peas she was saving—but I didn't dare ask. It was an unspoken rule that you didn't challenge Grandma when it came to either food or money.

My dad, like all of us, was a product of his upbringing; and even as he progressed in his career, he never lost that feeling of being on a farm worried about how the harvest would turn out. As a result, his money ethos was that you had to make every effort to spend as little as possible. He was a brilliant man, but he was that guy who would come home and brag about how much he saved driving from store to store comparison shopping for a relatively small item, even though he spent more on gas than the few dollars he saved. And we would use said item well past its expiration date. I remember a brush in particular that he used our entire childhood, long after it lost most of the bristles. Dad's brush was a source of great pride, especially laid against my mom's vanity table filled with her makeup and face creams. All he needed to groom himself was a single brush he bought in like 1969, which I'm not even sure he paid a full dollar for at that time. I wouldn't be surprised if he calculated what the brush cost him on a per day basis (after using it for decades). He was getting ready for his day for a *tiny fraction of a penny*! That was something to be very proud of in his mind. (Keep in mind he was naturally very good looking with the kind of hair that was just enough to cover his head but didn't exactly need extensive brushing or styling, so it's not like he needed much more than the brush he had. What stuck in the minds of all of us kids was how adamant he was to never waste money on a new brush. When it came down to it, we couldn't tell whether his hair was brushed or not, as he had good genes so he could roll out of bed ready for the day.)

Here's another story to further capture my dad's level of frugality. In the late summer of 1987, when I secured my long-awaited driver's license, I was allowed to drive the family car. It was a two-toned brown 1976 Caprice Classic Chevrolet that we called the "headache" car because of the gas fumes it emitted. I began to get increasingly worried about the brakes in particular, which were becoming less and less effective at actually stopping the car. Dad brushed my worries off, arguing that the car at that point only had a "few hundred thousand miles." (We didn't know how many, because once it hit 100,000, the odometer went back to zero, and no one knew how many times that occurred.) Dad kept reminding me that there was always an emergency brake that I could use as a backup. He would argue that, functionally, thanks to the emergency brake, the car could actually stop even if the regular brakes went out, and so the poor-performing brakes were nothing to worry about. At some point in the spring of 1989, I was driving—with my brother in the passenger seat—down a steep hill toward a stoplight when the brakes failed; lo and behold, dad was right. The emergency brake saved our lives that day! (He did *finally* buy a new car after that incident at my mom's insistence.)

MY MOM'S MONEY STORY

My mom watched her own dad progress from working as a milkman (back in the days when milk was delivered to your doorstep) to being the owner of three convenience stores, getting where he did through hard work, grit, and incredible people skills. Mom's family was able to move from working class to middle class over the course of her childhood, but was by no means wealthy. There was always a sense of uncertainty with my grandfather's business—and both he and my grandmother lived in a state of worry that they would somehow fall backward and lose it all, so money was a difficult subject, especially given the fact my grandmother liked to spend and my grandfather wanted to save. Between the two of them, they did progressively grow their net worth over time, but there was a lot of stress along the way, with my grandfather under constant pressure to outearn what my grandmother spent.

Once my mom's dad worked his way up from delivering milk to owning a small chain of convenience stores, my mom's mom made it her purpose to become part of Frankfort, Indiana, "society." My grand-parents joined the local country club, and they spent much of their money socializing with the other folks in Frankfort who had achieved similar status within their small town. For Grandmother (note she was "Grandmother"—you didn't dare call her "Grandma"), appearances were everything; and while my mom openly eschewed my grandmother's "showiness," she didn't fully escape it.

Mom was also a fan of keeping up appearances; and while she was careful in how much she spent, it was absolutely imperative that our family "show well," which meant everything from exhibiting the right manners, to having an immaculate house, to being well groomed and styled. For the manners, she sent us to charm school and enrolled us in endless activities designed to make us more educated and worldly. For the immaculate house, we had a live-in housekeeper, unheard of at the time when having a maid was considered a luxury. In terms of always being "presentable," while Mom didn't care about expensive labels, we were promptly taken to get new clothes and shoes when anything started to look too worn.

At the end of the day, though, Mom was also relatively frugal, just not at the expense of making sure our lives looked as perfect as possible to the outside world. Dad's brush drove her crazy, just as her cosmetics and closet of very presentable attire irked him; but their values ultimately skewed toward saving money, which made their marriage work more than it didn't from a financial perspective. They also both had a distinct bent toward investing. My dad saw that while his father was extremely careful with his money, his father also *had* to make critical investments to run the farm—to pay for tractors, workers, trucks to carry large amounts of produce to market, etc. My dad saw the distinction between investing in something that would ideally earn more money over time versus spending on "things," like a brush that had essentially no resale value (particularly his brush).

My mom, similarly, saw how her dad was able to use his sales skills to ultimately make enough money to buy a store, and then take some of the earnings from that store to buy another. And while there were tough years similar to those at the farm my dad grew up on, my mom recognized that without this investment, her family wouldn't have the comfortable middle-class life that her mother valued so much. My mom saw her dad go from working class to middle class through saving and investing, and that left an indelible impression.

And this is what I believe ultimately drove my mom to make the decision that would change our financial situation forever: to start one of the first educational software companies, Davidson & Associates, in the early 1980s. That company, started in an abandoned schoolroom, ultimately became a massive success; and by the time I was a senior in high school, my family had achieved what my grandparents never could imagine. We had "real money."

THE PIVOTAL MOMENT IN
OUR FAMILY'S FINANCIAL HISTORY

This is where it gets really interesting, though: Where I am today, and what I have been able to do with my life in creating Financial Finesse, came down to a very spirited debate over the dinner table. My mom had just started Davidson & Associates, and she and my dad had decided to use money they had saved for their children's college educations as seed capital to fund the expenses needed to bring the educational software the company was developing to market.

Both felt an obligation to ultimately return that money to us. The difference was that my mom wanted to take it as a low interest rate loan—and pay us back before college so there would be funds to cover at least some of our college education expenses. My dad had a very different idea. He wanted to give us shares in the company in exchange for tapping into the savings they'd put away for our college education. That way, we'd have a stake in the business, and it would truly be a family business, the way his family's farm was, where everyone was a part of the enterprise. They went back and forth and back and forth, but ultimately my dad prevailed.

That small stake (and it was a very small stake) ended up being worth a lot of money—enough money for me to not only start my own business, but live comfortably for the rest of my life. It was a complete and total game changer. My dad, without realizing it at the time, created opportunities for me that would have never otherwise existed. Indeed, I wouldn't be sitting here writing this book if my mom had won the argument.

Because the company my mom started took years to grow, it wasn't until after college that I fully realized the extent of what they had created. My parents at that point had created a trust, one that I couldn't touch until age 30 and couldn't fully access until I was 40. So I had an interesting paradox. Growing up, nothing felt different: My dad was still beyond frugal. And minus the luxuries my mom insisted on to keep up appearances—most notably our live-in housekeeper/babysitter who controlled the mess and chaos we kids created—we lived a pretty normal, suburban life. I went to public school; I never worried about going hungry but also never had an allowance; and any time I wanted something my mom wasn't ready to purchase for me, I paid for it with money I made working at my mom's company.

Like my dad's family farm, my mom's company, Davidson & Associates, really was a family endeavor. All of us kids worked in the business throughout our childhood, doing everything from stuffing envelopes, to working on the factory floor, to processing credit card transactions for those who called in to order the software. As I grew older, the jobs became more fun—like testing the software for bugs, running user labs to get feedback from prospective customers, or, better yet, making recommendations to the developers about how they could improve the user experience. I enjoyed the work, even the more repetitive tasks, because I felt like I was contributing, like I was doing something besides just "being a kid," which seemed pretty purposeless to me, especially as I got older. But there was also this deep sense of pride and ownership. This was not just my mom's business; my dad ultimately left a lucrative career as an executive at Parson's Corporation to join my mom in running the company, and my brother, sister, and I each had a stake in it. For all of us, how things turned out truly mattered, financially as shareholders of course, but also emotionally.

Even though I wasn't programming the software or selling it to stores, I felt a connection to the products and the children I imagined using them. I would look at a single package of software, and think I might have been the one to duplicate the disk (a process of taking a master copy and copying it on a disk that others could use to access it—remember this was pre-internet). Or maybe I shrink-wrapped the packaging or found bugs in the actual program that were subsequently fixed before it hit the shelves. Regardless, I felt a deep connection to the business, and like my mom did with her dad's convenience stores, I got to both participate in and watch the growth over time. From an early age, I knew deep down I would build a company of my own someday; it was that embedded in my psyche as a way of life—a natural progression of what I had experienced as a child, just like my mom following in her father's entrepreneurial footsteps.

MY MONEY STORY AND SCRIPT

So, put together my parents' stories of financial struggle in my dad's case and financial progress but uncertainty in my mom's case, add in my situation of being a small partial owner in a company that I spent my childhood doing odd jobs for and ultimately benefited financially from, and what you get is the money script that I unconsciously inherited.

From my parents' example and their own money scripts passed on by their parents, the messages came through loud and clear:

- **Spend wisely and on things that really matter to you, ideally things that grow in value over time or that you feel are really important to your quality of life.** This has been a great gift, and I've kept it.

- **The best way to grow your wealth is to build a business.** (Not necessarily true when you look at national statistics, but based on my family's experience, that was the obvious conclusion.)

- **Save as much as possible, don't be pretentious (from my dad), and be presentable always (from my mom).** This caused uneasiness for me for years—hearing my mom's voice in my head criticizing me for not being "pulled together" and hearing my dad's voice in my head criticizing me for what I did spend on the outfit or the venue or whatever it was.

- **Money is something you have to *earn*, and it really only counts if your own efforts generate it.** This fostered a good work ethic but also a sense of guilt for any time I ever got lucky when it came to money, whether that was a new client we acquired without having to go through a grueling sales process or an investment I made that skyrocketed. I always felt that for money to really "count" and for me to have a sense of accomplishment, the money had to be hard won, and that caused me to subconsciously avoid easier ways to make money. So instead I would pursue things that were unreasonably difficult so I could look back and feel like I truly earned whatever came of that endeavor.

- **Money is a measure of your success in life.** Because my parents came from nothing and built one of the most successful businesses of their time, that's what real success looked like to me. For years, I measured myself against their financial success, well aware that I had a leg up because of the stock I had from their company, which allowed me to fund my own. That fueled my motivation to succeed, which I am grateful for, but in the process, I put far too much pressure on myself as a result—and I think that clouded my judgment at times.

■ **Those who are fortunate (like myself) have an obligation to help others less fortunate.** Because of my luck, I felt compelled to give back, level the playing field, and help others become financially secure themselves. I'm very glad about this part—it gave me my purpose—but the purpose came with a compulsion as well, and I far too often worked to the detriment of my personal life.

While my parents generally instilled positive values about money in all their children, my money script had some serious flaws that held me back. I spent most of my adult life trying to measure up to the success they had achieved, always using money as a "score" of sorts. While I was very fortunate to not have to deal with the kind of financial stress most people face (at least once I turned 30 and was able to tap into money from my shares in my parents' company), I was constantly scrambling to achieve financial goals, personally and for my company, that weren't attainable. I would then berate myself for not achieving them, which would usually result in my doubling down and working harder, at a cost to my personal life and mental health. Here I was, running a successful, mission-based company that was helping people transform their lives, and I wasn't able to appreciate any of it. I was lucky enough to live my purpose, but all the benefits that came from that—the sense of pride, fulfillment, and joy— were missing, replaced by a feeling of never quite being "good enough." I also grappled with feeling like a fraud because, thanks to my parent's success and their dinner table decision to give my brother, sister, and me a stake in the amazing business they created, I didn't have financial challenges myself and yet was dedicating my life to helping other people overcome theirs.

It took years not only to realize the flaws in my money script, but to build and live by a healthier one that has made me a happier, more fulfilled human being (and a better wife, mother, friend, and boss).

My new money script goes something like this:

■ Money is fuel to live the most meaningful, purposeful life I am capable of living and to provide opportunities for as many people as possible to be able to achieve the same.

- Money is not a score to measure against. I don't need to equal or exceed my parents' success to feel that I've been a success. Instead I choose to define success by the quality of relationships I have with those I love, the impact I have on their lives, and my ability to help as many people as possible, as meaningfully as possible within my career. No longer is there a financial component attached to my idea of success, though I still recognize that the more we make as an organization, the more we can reinvest into expanding to help more people. So, again, it's still fuel—just not self-worth!

- I choose to spend my money on the things that I feel create the best life for myself, my family, and the larger world based on causes I donate to. Anyone looking at my budget would be appalled at how little I spend in certain areas and how much in others, but I'm very happy with the results because I'm using my money in a way that I feel has the most impact and creates the most fulfilling lives for myself and those I care most about in the world.

- I'm a work in progress, with the prerogative to change my mind as my life changes, as my priorities evolve, and as I learn more about how I can make best use of the money I have. I'm also going to make mistakes—what may feel like a good idea at one time in my life (one particular tattoo comes to mind) will not later. And that's the nature of being human. You grow, learn, and evolve as a person, and also in the way you manage, spend, save, and invest your money. This is how it should be, and I no longer punish myself for decisions that seem stupid in retrospect. All we can do is our best, and if we pay attention to the lessons life gives us, our best becomes better over time.

HOW REVISING YOUR MONEY SCRIPT CAN CHANGE YOUR LIFE

While my money story is unique, the emotions I felt around money were not. Even though I had more than enough, it wasn't enough until I revised my script. Whether you are financially struggling, in a strong financial position like I was but still stressed about money, or somewhere in the middle where you beat yourself up because you aren't "further along" in life, you probably have a money script that needs to be examined and revised.

When you take back control of how you think about and view money, it truly is life-changing. First of all, you really do turn money into fuel to build the life you want. But you also achieve financial freedom faster because you stop making emotional financial decisions that don't serve you. Even saving as little $1, $3, or $5 per day—by saving, spending, and investing more intentionally in line with your values—can ultimately transform your finances, turning small amounts into hundreds of thousands or even millions of dollars over your lifetime. More importantly, you can do so without a feeling of angst, stress, sacrifice, regret, or shame. You can look back and be proud of the decisions you've made and how they've influenced your life—and the lives of those you care most about—for the better.

EXERCISE

Transform Your Money Script So It Supports Your Financial Success

Here are five steps you can take to ultimately transform your money script and put it into action:

1. Just as you did at the beginning of the chapter, think of all the recent financial events that have happened in your life and how you responded—everything as small as the things you tell yourself when you pay your bills or view your account or credit balances to things as big as major financial emergencies or financial windfalls you didn't anticipate. Write down how you reacted and include the story you told yourself about why these events occurred, what they meant to your finances and overall life, and how you decided to address them (or paradoxically, not to address them if you either felt hopeless or immediately went into denial mode, telling yourself that the situation would somehow fix itself).

2. Determine the patterns from these events to get to a starting point for your current money script.

3. To further understand what is driving your money script so you can change it as needed, think about the people in your life who helped you shape your attitudes about money. They may have done this by virtue of the financial habits and behaviors they modeled, their relationships with money that seeped through in the messages they sent you, or the lessons they taught you directly about the best way to manage your money. How did their influence play out in your money script? How entrenched are they as part of your core values, your sense of self-identity, the way you have chosen to live your life?

4. To create a more positive money script, look at everything you've written down and determine what serves your financial success and what you'll want to change.

5. Put your new money script to use to the point where it becomes your default—or automatic—way of thinking about money. This change will be hard, and it may take as long as several months to a year to become ingrained in your subconscious. Ironically, to get there, the best thing you can do is be as conscious as possible about applying your new money script to the different financial situations and decisions you face on a daily basis. My team and I have found that people tend to be the most successful when they actually write their script down; laminate it if possible to make it more "official"; and make it easily accessible, in their wallet, for example, so they can pull it out as a reminder as needed. In the beginning of this process, most people have to fight to adhere to their new money script, but over time, the new money script becomes increasingly powerful until it ultimately replaces their old money script. At that point, they no longer need the reminder. They have successfully changed their money script for the better, and it will be running in the background guiding their decision-making in a much more productive way!

3

CREATE YOUR FINANCIAL IDENTITY

After you've identified and revised your money script to align better with your values, so that you aren't held hostage by subconscious beliefs that don't serve your financial security or your long-term happiness, the next step is to form a financial identity. For the vast majority of people we coach, the concept of having a financial identity is completely foreign. They are accustomed to the concept of identifying with a religion, a political party, or a specific diet or healthy lifestyle, but when it comes to finances, identity is uncharted territory.

It is also a major missed opportunity, because forming a financial identity is one of the most important things you can do to both achieve and maintain financial success. It unlocks something that even the best technology can't accomplish—that is to automate how you make financial decisions in line with your true values. This sets you up to use money as fuel to live and build the life you want instead of getting sucked into the temptation to spend money on what feels good in the moment, but has no bearing on what truly matters to you.

When you establish a firm financial identity and integrate it into your life, it not only becomes how you live, but also embodies *who you are* as a person. Our financial coaches have found that getting people to automate themselves by establishing a financial identity is often the most pivotal financial turning point in the coaching process—where people really start to gain momentum and entirely change the trajectory of their future. Why? Because, by nature, we tend to be motivated to stay true to our convictions and, more importantly, to be accountable to them. You see this all the time when people attach their identity to a specific religious dogma, nutrition plan, or political agenda. Their beliefs compel them to act in a way that conforms to their identity. And with that level of consistency comes automation. When you establish a financial identity, you become intentional—predeciding how you are going to manage your money, and maybe, more importantly, how you aren't. This is a natural extension to your money script. The money script gives you a guiding light for making financial decisions that align with your values and keep your subconscious focused on your "why," so you make decisions through a lens that advances your life. But even when you have a highly intentional money script, there are still so many decisions to be made, that it's easy to get derailed and end up rationalizing how your decisions fit into your script when, in reality, they aren't serving you the way you tell yourself they are.

When you combine your money script with a financial identity that you've chosen to live by, you reduce the distraction of choices that may not be right for you long term, because anything that does not align with your financial identity becomes off-limits, the way that someone following a specific healthy lifestyle, say choosing to go gluten-free will automatically screen out any and all food that contains gluten. It's not even a choice at that point. You can do the same thing with finances by forming a financial identity that not only eliminates the temptation to make decisions at odds with the identity you've adopted, but ensures that your brain doesn't even contemplate them as a reasonable possibility!

Our team at Financial Finesse has created six different financial identities based on our experience helping millions of people transform their finances. These identities are listed below. As you read through each of the identities, really think about each one and consider which most aligns with your values so you can make a commitment to following the one you choose. Please keep in mind that it is very likely none of the identities will fit you perfectly. That's completely normal. The idea is to pick the financial identity that will be easiest to integrate into your life so you can stick to it without having to make major sacrifices that compromise your sense of joy, fulfillment, and satisfaction in life. Also, you may discover as you go through different phases of your life that it's worth revisiting the identity you chose and picking one that better fits your priorities at that time. For example, people who start with an Investor identity often migrate to a Giver identity as they age and begin to think about leaving a legacy. Those with a Bargain Hunter identity may reach a point where bargain hunting is no longer fun, or they don't have the time to invest in it and decide to adopt an Automator identity instead.

FINANCIAL IDENTITY TYPE 1: THE INVESTOR

I know this one best because it happens to be my own financial identity. It essentially means that you spend money with an investment mindset—trying to put as much money as possible into things that are going to grow financially in value *or* are truly going to provide you and your loved ones with a better life through opportunities, experiences, or convenience.

This is how having a financial identity as an *investor* has played out in my life:

I don't spend a lot of money on "things" that are going to depreciate in value, like clothes, cars, or electronics for entertainment. (In all three cases, I wait until they are completely worn out and no longer functional before I buy a replacement.) However, I will *invest* in technology that makes my life more convenient or enables me to work more productively.

I will also invest in once-in-a-lifetime experiences, especially with family, where I feel like we are making memories that will last a lifetime. Even though I can't sell those investments for a profit, I consider them to be investments because they have an enduring impact on the people I love most.

That said, my general MO is to spend as little as possible on things that are going to decline in value and to find ways to avoid replacing these items by getting creative—for example, mixing and matching my wardrobe to keep it fresh as opposed to buying new clothes, getting nice heels repaired rather than replacing them, or borrowing jewelry from friends for the rare occasions I wear any, in exchange for lending them things they would rather use once or twice than purchase themselves.

This may sound really cheap to many of you—and I can see that perspective—but I would argue it's more nuanced than that—or maybe I just don't want to be called cheap! Seriously, in my mind, it's not about hoarding money to my own detriment or going to absurd extremes to save a few pennies at the expense of my time and sanity. Instead it's about making sure that I can channel as much money as possible into items that will grow over time—such as real estate, art, collectibles, antiques, and, of course, more traditional investments.

Because investors are always aware of what's important to them, spending decisions become much easier. Because I know this is my financial identity, I can go into a car dealership with a modest car-buying budget, immediately find a car that best suits my needs (which are safety and durability so it will last as long as possible!), and walk away satisfied. I'm not at all tempted by the red Corvette in the center of the showroom floor because I know the minute I drive it off the lot, it will lose most of its value, and that makes me so uncomfortable, it's not even an option I would entertain.

In this sense, my financial identity as an investor puts me in a position where I automatically predecide how I'm going to use my money, and maybe, more importantly, what I will never use my money for without making a conscious decision that requires restraint and willpower. That feeling of not having to wrestle with yourself over whether or not you purchase something is incredibly freeing and ends up paying off in the long term in the form of ensuring you use your money on things that matter to you.

Signs You Are a Natural Investor

- **You are future-oriented.** In my (and my team's) experience, people are oriented in one of three ways: past, present, or future. People who are past-oriented heavily lean on the past to make financial decisions. People who are present-oriented focus on what they need to do in the moment to satisfy their financial needs. People who are future-oriented look at how the money they spend today will impact their future. Investors are inherently future-oriented people, not just with money but with life in general. If people all your life have told you that you are great at thinking ahead, or even that you think too far ahead or "get ahead of yourself," you are probably future-oriented.

- **You are a big-picture thinker.** You are not focused on details as much as making sure you are progressing on the things you feel make the biggest impact on your life, relationship, career, or family.

- **You are bottom-line-oriented versus process-oriented.** You are much more focused on the end result than the process it will take to get there.

- **You live by the mantra "progress over perfection."** Investors are thoughtful in their decision-making, but they aren't prone to overanalyze decisions, even large ones. They see their time as an investment in and of itself, and have a natural understanding of "diminishing returns"—meaning that they are not obsessed with finding the cheapest price no matter what, or spending undue time to pick the absolute best possible investment at the risk of losing the window of opportunity to make a good investment.

- **You are independent—less subject than most to peer pressure.** Investors care much more about the long-term future they are building than the fads of the moment. They don't feel a need to be "on trend" from a fashion and lifestyle perspective— and really don't care that others may judge them for this. This allows them to focus almost exclusively on what they feel will serve them financially because they don't see the need to "keep up appearances."

Being an investor may sound like a great identity in terms of what you can achieve long term, but it is only the right identity for you if you are naturally inclined toward it to begin with. After all, the point of adopting a financial identity is to solidify a lifestyle that is in line with both your personality and your values. Otherwise, it won't stick. And what makes the most impact on long-term financial success is having a consistent way of managing and growing your money that you cannot only stick to, but fit seamlessly into your life without you even having to think about it.

FINANCIAL IDENTITY TYPE 2: BARGAIN HUNTER

Bargain hunters love doing what many of us hate—spending inordinate amounts of time to get the best deal possible on the purchases they make. They also fully leverage the opportunity to ultimately get things for "free"—for example, earning points or miles when traveling, joining friends on their vacation in exchange for babysitting their children or playing the role of tour guide if it's an area they are familiar with, promoting products on social media in exchange for getting them free, or becoming a product tester for the same reason.

Bargain hunters are also exceptional at understanding and maximizing their employer benefits. They take advantage of employer paid benefits and resources that most of us might not even be aware of—from commuter benefits, to free legal assistance through their employee assistance program or prepaid legal benefit, to tuition reimbursement, to career development opportunities to attain certifications in their field that ultimately increase their earning potential. Their mantra is never to pay more than they need to, and never to pay at all if something is available free of charge. Similar to the way many people view the investor identity, people also initially think this means bargain hunters are frugal to the point of deprivation. That's not the case at all. They don't eschew buying things that add enjoyment to their lives. They simply love the process of figuring out how to do so as cost-effectively as possible. And in doing so, they not only have fun but free up money to save and invest for their future and ultimately achieve greater levels of financial freedom.

Signs You Are a Natural Bargain Hunter

- **You get a rush out of getting a deal.** It is fun for you to find clever ways to get things free of charge or at a heavily discounted rate. You enjoy taking the extra time to find the best possible price.
- **You likely have both a love and skill for negotiating.** While others may find the process anxiety producing or exhausting, you find it rewarding and usually get the result you want—or at least come close.
- **The concept of paying "full retail" makes you cringe.** You avoid expensive shops, not because you don't like their merchandise, but because you know there must be a way to get the same things for much less.
- **You love figuring out how to game a system to get the most out of it.** You read the fine print on coupons, credit card rewards programs, memberships, and mileage programs that airlines provide so that you can maximize the amount of perks you get free of charge.
- **You love flea markets, garage sales, and estate sales.** You have an innate ability to find items that have significant value among the clutter of stuff that is being sold.

Again, if it sounds exhausting to spend this level of time and energy into always getting the best deal, then this is not a financial identity you should adopt. It simply won't fit into your lifestyle, and you'll become irritated with the process and will give up because it taxes your energy and willpower, instead of bringing you enjoyment. And that's OK. While we all are subject to the forces of human nature, each one of us is unique in what works for us and the way we live. The key, as I said earlier, is picking an identity that naturally works for you—not trying to change yourself to conform to an identity because you think you "should" operate that way.

FINANCIAL IDENTITY TYPE 3: MINIMALIST

This one is probably the easiest to self-identify. If you are a minimalist, chances are you know it and are already living mostly in line with this identity. The key is staying true to it and not feeling pressure to question or change the way you live to conform to others in your life who may give you a hard time for eschewing a more luxurious lifestyle. There are endless ways to nourish relationships without having to spend money doing so. Two of my favorite people, a husband-and-wife couple, embody this identity and have managed to maintain incredible relationships with people who have vastly different financial sensibilities without compromising their own.

They became financially secure in their forties by living a simple but deeply fulfilling life doing what they loved (creating beautiful wooden art pieces). For years, they lived in a cabin on an island outside of Seattle, with the bare essentials and only a few modern conveniences. Their days were filled with long hikes, camping, singing around the campfire, reading, and getting together with like-minded friends and family who could just hang out and enjoy the beauty that surrounded them on their acres of property. They grew their own food, made many of their own clothes, and lived the happiest, most fulfilled lives I've ever known two people to have. While I'm not a minimalist myself, some of my favorite memories are being with them in a beautiful setting, getting out of the rat race and simply enjoying the present. Our relationship was richer for the fact they were minimalists, because of the influence their lifestyle had on me, and the same was true for other friends and family members who knew them. They served as a source of inspiration, and wherever they were, you knew they felt the pleasure of each other's company. And they always brought with them a feeling of home and a reminder to enjoy the beauty of nature.

If you are someone who loves the simple pleasures in life and feels that material things detract from your enjoyment of it, you are incredibly lucky. Not only are you likely to have a more peaceful and spiritual existence than the rest of us, but you are also likely to become financially secure early in life, giving you more time to pursue your passions and purpose. To you, it's no sacrifice not to own the latest electronics, and you couldn't care less what's in fashion at the moment. In fact, on the rare occasions when your friends or relatives drag you to an expensive store, you can simply marvel at the rest of us buying things we don't need (sometimes with money we don't actually have). You don't consciously decide not to spend money on the things the rest of us covet—it's simply what you do by default, because it's part of who you are.

Signs You Are a Minimalist

- **You live in the present and cherish the moments with those you love above all else.** Where you are or even what you are doing takes a backseat to those you are with and how much you are enjoying their company.
- **You aren't chained to your phone.** You use your phone as a utility to communicate with others as needed, but you don't consider it to be central to having a satisfying life.
- **You are happiest entertaining friends and family** at home or spending time in nature.
- **You don't typically get very tied to physical possessions unless they are sentimental in nature**—and you tend to have a "what's mine is yours" philosophy when it comes to letting people use or borrow your possessions.
- **People have always commented on how "low maintenance" you are.** You are likely the person who gets ready quickly, packs very light for a trip, and easily adapts to most situations even when they don't go as planned.

- **You are not a fan of social media.** You may have accounts to keep up with others, but you'd much rather be spending time with people and enjoying the moment than documenting it.

FINANCIAL IDENTITY TYPE 4: THE PLANNER

This is my late grandma, who lived through the Great Depression, was the oldest of six siblings, and took on the role of caregiver when her own mom died in childbirth. With all these circumstances and the unpredictability of living on a farm that the family depended on for both food and income, she turned to planning as much as she could as a form of maintaining a semblance of control in her often difficult, chaotic world.

Every time Grandma went to the store, she had a list of everything she wanted to buy, and she adamantly *refused* to buy anything not on the list. She sometimes took this to an extreme, not allowing herself wiggle room to buy items she had forgotten to put on the list. She would literally return home and create an entirely new list whenever this happened, then return to the store to buy the items she forgot on the first list!

But at the end of the day, she was one of the most financially savvy people I ever met. It took many decades, but this humble farmer's wife eventually became a millionaire by taking the money she didn't spend on what she called "frivolous items" and instead investing it. There was also a plan for investing—which until the very end of her life, when she became a victim of fraud, she stuck to religiously. Grandma always thought about the goal at hand, whether short term or long term, and then created a detailed plan to get there. The thought of straying from that was intolerable to her, and while some would criticize her lack of flexibility, it served her incredibly well in the long run and set a powerful example for her children and grandchildren. While most of us didn't adopt a planner identity outright, Grandma's lessons became part of our money scripts—to make sure we used our money thoughtfully and wisely based on our goals.

Signs You Are a Planner

- **When you are in a group, people automatically look to you to arrange, communicate, and follow plans.** When you are with people you know well, this typically happens naturally, without you or anyone else "appointing" you as the leader.
- **You love to-do lists** and that tremendous feeling of satisfaction that comes from completing and subsequently crossing off items on your to-do lists.
- **You feel most comfortable when you are in control** of important situations, from making the big decisions all the way down to completing the details.
- **If things don't go according to plan,** you create a new plan as a way of adapting versus simply reacting to the situation in the moment.
- **And maybe most significantly, planning is fun—sometimes more fun even than actually doing what you plan!** You look forward to making plans; it gives you a sense of joy, purpose, and excitement.

FINANCIAL IDENTITY TYPE 5: THE GIVER

Givers are the altruistic people who get much more joy from helping others than improving their own personal financial situation. They prioritize spending and investing in opportunities that add real value to the lives of their loved ones and contribute a good deal of their money to charity, feeling this is the way they can make a difference in the world. Givers are the parents who will work overtime to pay for the best possible education for their children, sacrificing significant material comforts if needed to afford the tuition. By the same token, they tend to care very little about their own image and spend minimal amounts on things they don't feel matter in the larger scheme of things—from fashion to jewelry to cars to nice vacations—really, all the trappings other people find so important. Givers get tremendous satisfaction from being able to provide for others in deeply impactful ways—using their money to literally change lives.

In fact, they see that as the real purpose of money, beyond providing for their own basic needs; and when they are able to use their money to make a difference, they are at their happiest and most fulfilled.

Signs You Are a Giver

- **Your default is to think of other people's needs** before your own, and you have to remind yourself to take care of yourself.
- **You naturally connect your level of success to the impact you have** on others.
- **You are deeply invested in specific causes** and feel compelled to do what you can, with both your money and your time, to support these causes.
- **Your greatest source of joy is watching those you love thrive,** and you feel the purpose of having money is to provide them with opportunities to create the lives that give them the greatest level of satisfaction and fulfillment.

FINANCIAL IDENTITY TYPE 6: THE AUTOMATOR

Automators value efficiency and simplicity. They gravitate toward setting up a system they can automatically employ to build financial security as opposed to agonizing over how to spend, save, and invest their money. They want their finances on autopilot because that frees up mind space for them to focus on other things that provide them with a greater sense of fun and fulfillment.

One of our financial coaches manages his money this way. He doesn't want to actively budget or agonize over whether he can afford something or not. Instead he directs his paycheck to different accounts to ensure that he's automatically saving and investing for his future, while still funding his wants and needs. He essentially has three separate "buckets" for his money:

- **Money he sets aside for his future** (he's big on having a big financial cushion, so for him it's 30 percent of his income;

but we've worked with others who have started considerably lower out of necessity, ramping up over time as their income and ability to save increased). He puts some of this money into his 401(k), which he maxes out for the company match, tax savings, and low-cost investments; he puts some of it into his HSA (health savings account), which he also maxes out because an HSA allows you to invest for future healthcare expenses without paying taxes on the earnings; and some of it goes into a Roth IRA, where he can withdraw what he's put into the account at any time in the event he has an emergency he needs to fund.

- **Money for necessary expenses** such as the mortgage, utilities, gas for his car, his Wi-Fi plan—the things he needs to live and work, which generally are either fixed or relatively easy to estimate.

- **Money for fun.** When his "money for fun" account starts to get low, he pulls back as needed, until the account gets automatically re-funded out of his next paycheck. It may seem like he's living paycheck to paycheck, but given that he's got a robust savings and investment account and that his fixed expenses are always covered, the system is doing a nice job increasing his net worth over time.

Signs You Are an Automator

- **You look for the easiest way to reach a goal, in all areas of your life, and are probably already automating key areas of your life to make that happen.** You use technology or systems to make it as easy as possible to accomplish what you want without thinking about it.

- **You love to "set it and forget it," knowing that if you set up the right system up front, the long term will take care of itself.** You do not obsess over declines in the market or worry when you have an emergency and need to tap into your savings, because you know you set up a system that will weather these events.

- **You are incredibly bottom-line-oriented, with a lack of interest in the play-by-play or the details.** To you, it's all about where you end up that matters. For example, when someone is telling a story, especially if you have a vested interest in the outcome, you want to hear the ending first. You find yourself asking people to get to the point regularly and find yourself checking out of the conversation if they take too long to do so.

- **You loathe wasting time.** You want to spend as little time as possible even thinking about money so you can free your time up for things that matter more.

- **The thought of having to track each expense feels like a form of torture,** especially if you have a system in place to ensure you are able to pay for your expenses, without compromising your future.

EXERCISE

Forming Your Own Financial Identity

If you are like most people we coach, you are probably thinking that you relate to multiple financial identities. The goal is to find the one that resonates most with you, and make a commitment to that one, understanding that you get to decide how to shape it so it fits your life. For example, if you are a *minimalist*, you don't have to forgo all comforts and conveniences. You don't have to go off the grid or live in a tiny house. You don't have to live without modern conveniences. You can simply decide that you want to live a relatively modest lifestyle and focus your enjoyment on the things that money can't buy—like time in nature, or quality time with your friends and family where you really get to enjoy each other's company instead of going on expensive trips. If you are an *investor* like me, you still can buy a new pair of shoes rather than have your shoes repaired when they break (I only do this for expensive shoes that actually can be restored to their original quality). And it's OK to pay for that expensive bridesmaid's dress even if you don't see it as a good financial "investment" because you'll never want to wear it again. You get to define what being an investor means, as long as you follow the spirit of the identity, which is to prioritize spending money on things that either grow in value over time or are an important investment in your own growth, relationships, and personal fulfillment. (And one could very much argue that buying that expensive but ugly dress is a critical investment in one of your most important friendships!)

So with all this in mind, here's your assignment:

1. **Go back and review each identity to see if you can commit to one of them.** If you look at any these identities and think, "Of all the identities, this best aligns with my values, and I can live following its key tenets and be happier and more fulfilled in the long run," then it's best to make a commitment to that identity and use it as your guiding light, knowing you can determine how to best integrate it into your life as opposed to following it in its most extreme form.

2. **If you can't make a commitment to any one identity because doing so requires eliminating things that are really important to you in life, but achieving financial independence is one of your most important goals, reconsider the automator identity.** This identity is naturally flexible since it allows you to spend money the way you want as long as you meet your long-term savings goals.

3. **Similar to your money script, you will need to actively practice following your identity until it becomes automatic.** To do this, I recommend you use the same approach you do with your money script—put your identity and its key tenets in writing, ideally on a laminated card in your wallet, and pull

the card out when you need to remind yourself of your values before you make a purchase. Over time, you won't need to do this—because your identity will be so ingrained, you won't even contemplate spending your money in a way that doesn't align with it.

4

USING YOUR BRIGHT
SPOTS TO ACHIEVE
FINANCIAL FREEDOM
EVEN FASTER

Once you've identified and revised your money script and solidi-
fied your financial identity, you are ready to take the last step
in the process of setting yourself up for financial success. This
step is based on an incredibly powerful concept, one that defies the conventional wisdom that our failure provides much better lessons than successes. It's called the "bright spot" concept.

The bright spot concept was discovered by brothers Dan and Chip
Heath, two PhDs in behavioral economics and authors of the bestsell-
ing book *Switch*. Dan and Chip conducted large-scale research studies
to determine the best way to solve seemingly unsolvable problems. And
that's how they discovered the incredible power of bright spots—which
are patterns that drive repeatable success. It's a concept that applies to
both individuals and groups.

You can discover bright spots when you look at instances where people or teams prevailed despite overwhelming odds—where they managed to succeed where others have failed or managed to overcome adversity that previously seemed insurmountable. Too often, we don't even register the importance of these triumphs, let alone what they can teach us. Left unexamined, many may even seem like "luck." But when Dan and Chip studied bright spots at scale—looking at thousands of examples across organizations and individuals—they discovered that in virtually all cases, there were underlying reasons for the breakthrough that could be replicated over and over again to get the same exceptional result. Here's what they found: Typically it was a combination of small things that made a huge difference.

In their book *Switch*, Dan and Chip Heath use the example of Jerry Sternin and his effort to reduce childhood malnutrition in Vietnam. In 1990 Sternin was working for Save the Children and had been invited to the country by the government. But when he arrived, he learned that not everyone was excited about his project and that he had six months to make a difference. He didn't speak the language and only had a small team. From his extensive research he knew that he and his team faced many huge problems such as sanitation, universal poverty, lack of clean water, nutritional ignorance, etc., that could never be solved in six months. Out of necessity, Sternin adopted a strategy of seeking out bright spots to determine what was working and how he could apply those learnings more broadly to make a difference as quickly as possible.

Sternin went out into local communities and created teams of mothers to weigh all the children. He then looked for examples of very poor children that were well nourished. After interviewing the families of these bright spots, he learned that a few basic adjustments made a huge difference. Though the societal norm was for children to eat high-quality rice twice a day with their families, and to judge on their own how much they needed, Sternin learned that meals were somewhat different in the households of bright spot children. The mothers in those households took a more active role, often hand-feeding their children. They also spread the same amount of food out over four meals and mixed in tiny shrimp, crab, and sweet potato greens (often considered a low-class food). With these findings, his team organized local community cooking classes, where mothers taught each other how to make tasty meals that included all the ingredients and how to best feed their children. Six months after Sternin's visit, 65 percent of children were better nourished and stayed that way!

In *Switch*, Dan and Chip Heath share dozens of examples of how to use bright spots to discover and apply what is working, but one of the most poignant, and I believe most relevant, comes down to a single story of the impact that bright spots had on a troubled student. I love this example because it brings it down to the individual level—which is what you will ultimately need to do to identify and leverage your own bright spots to accelerate your financial progress. Here's a short summary of the story:

> John J. Murphy, a high school psychologist, was facing serious challenges with a troubled ninth grader named Bobby. Several teachers had referred Bobby to John, as Bobby was constantly late, rarely did his work, was disruptive in class, and sometimes made loud threats to other students in the hallways. Bobby also had a rough home life. He'd been shuffled in and out of foster homes and special facilities for children with behavioral problems. John really had his work cut out for him, as he didn't have consistent access to Bobby; just an hour here and there.
>
> He started by asking Bobby, "Tell me about the times at school when you don't get in trouble as much." Bobby mentioned that he seemed to get in trouble much less in Ms. Smith's class. After several more questions, refusing to move on until Bobby had given specific answers, John discovered that Bobby benefited from how Ms. Smith always greeted him as soon as he walked into class, catered his work to his learning style, and always made sure he understood the instructions. John decided to see what happened if

Bobby's other teachers adopted the same approach. Would it make the difference he hoped?

John approached Bobby's other teachers and gave them these three specific suggestions. He also asked them to help him track Bobby's progress in terms of arriving to class on time, completing assignments in class, and behaving acceptably in class.

The teachers, desperate to help Bobby and also reduce his disruption in class, immediately implemented all three suggestions. The results defied logic! After just three months, Bobby's frequency of being reported to the office for a major infraction decreased 80 percent. He also made striking progress in the three areas of focus, with his teachers rating his behavior as acceptable four or five out of six classes per day versus only one or two before the changes. Big problems don't always need big solutions. By finding the bright spots and trying to replicate them, small changes can have a huge impact!

So what does Bobby's story have to do with improving your finances? Well, it turns out that we all have times we triumphed against the odds and overcame challenges we initially felt were nearly impossible, and that by examining these successes, we can find our own bright spots and use them to achieve seemingly impossible financial goals. Our triumphs may be financial in nature; others may be accomplishing daunting goals, like running a marathon, saving our marriage and ending up with a stronger relationship than we ever had, advocating for our children and securing opportunities for them that we were initially told were simply not available, overcoming depression or other mental health challenges, or succeeding at any other number of things that at first seemed impossible but where we managed to find a way to prevail.

My team and I have recently begun a fascinating research project, interviewing people we've coached to learn more about exactly how they overcame financial challenges. Obviously, the coaching played a major role, but coaching is clearly not the only factor. While most people make some improvement in their finances after going through financial coaching, the scale of that improvement varies. Virtually everyone starts out motivated and determined, but many ultimately fall into old habits and behaviors, which either slows or completely halts their long-term progress. But then there are those superstars who not only progress but completely change the way they think about and use money; they end up going from being financially stressed with high levels of debt and challenges making ends meet to becoming financially secure with significant savings and investments, generally within one to two years.

It turns out that the vast majority of these superstars had internalized their own bright spots, taking what worked for them to achieve success in other areas of their lives and applying it to their finances. At some point in our interviews, they almost invariably shared the lessons they learned about "what works for them" and how they actively applied these lessons to their finances. This goes beyond refining their money scripts and forming a financial identity (which most had done as well). It's more that they detected patterns in their own successes—their bright spots—and carried them forward to create incredible momentum that enabled them to achieve financial security much faster than their peers.

The patterns were very individualized. Some people discovered they were at their best when they found ways to get perspective, remind themselves of their end goals, and find a way to track progress. Others discovered that they were most successful when they created a mantra they could keep front and center of their mind to focus on the things they could control and let go of those they couldn't, sharing their mantra with their families and friends for accountability and reinforcement. Still others discovered that they were most successful in life and with their finances when they created a very clear vision—sometimes even storyboarding what their goals were and placing the board in an area where they were forced to see it every day; they would then track and celebrate their progress toward achieving their ultimate vision, understanding they needed both the big-picture "why" and the small victories to be successful. The bottom line is that virtually all had figured out what worked for them and had actively integrated those things into their lives.

THE FIVE KEY AREAS TO CONSIDER WHEN IDENTIFYING YOUR OWN BRIGHT SPOTS

At the end of the day, most people's bright spots fit into the following five categories, which brain science researchers have discovered are critical to setting yourself up not just for financial success, but for success in any other area of your life. My hope is that in reading through these, you'll make connections between how each of these areas has influenced your success in the past and can be used to supercharge your financial success going forward.

Motivation

As you go through the process of identifying your own bright spots, look for what motivated you to achieve your successes. Motivation is a universal human requirement to have the fortitude to stick through the difficulties we face when we try to make significant changes, but *how* we are motivated is a very individual thing. For some people, it's regularly revisiting their why and reminding themselves of the importance of the work they are doing. Some become motivated when they surround themselves with people who have overcome similar challenges and are a deep source of inspiration. For others, it's creating a good life for their children that keeps them going when times get hard. Still others seek out inspiration in the form of TED Talks or events where exceptional people get together to share both their challenges and victories. To increase your chances of sticking with your plans when times get hard, you need to figure out what motivates you and make sure you consciously pursue those things so that you don't ever lose sight of why you are doing the hard work needed to make meaningful progress.

TIM'S STORY

Motivation sometimes happens without your seeking it, due to a life event. Tim, 42, called the Financial Coaching Line at Financial Finesse because he was witnessing how damaging financial stress was to his marriage. Despite making a good living as a technology salesperson at the top of his profession, his spending outpaced his earnings—even though he was making progressively more money each year. His wife, Julie, who worked as a marketing manager for a nonprofit she loved, was increasingly dipping into her 401(k) to help him pay credit card bills, draining her wealth. She finally reached a breaking point when Tim suggested she quit the job she loved and get a job at a financial services company his friend worked at, which paid a considerably higher salary. He seemingly forgot that she had intentionally left financial services marketing years ago because she found it "soul-sucking." This was the final straw for Julie, who was already sick of funding his spending habits from her 401(k). She flipped the script on him and told him that unless he found a way to get his finances under control, she would leave.

And that was exactly the motivation Tim needed. Nothing was worth losing his wife, but the motivation was bigger than that: He wanted to be a better husband to Julie, once he realized how much he had already damaged their relationship; he knew that she deserved that and that he did as well. He was capable of doing better and determined to prove that to himself and his wife.

To save his marriage and become the husband his wife deserved, Tim called our coaching line with his wife, and they had meetings every week with a financial coach for three years. During that time, they not only paid all Tim's debt off, but ultimately restored what Julie had lost in her 401(k) and then some. Whenever Tim resisted changes that the coach suggested or backslid into a spending binge, the coach reinforced how important these changes were to his marriage and reminded him of his commitment to do better for the sake of his future with Julie, bringing him back to his motivation. Ultimately, that was enough for him to get back on track and build upon the positive changes he made.

Accountability

Chances are your bright spots also include some sort of accountability. All the research on what drives lasting change shows that the more you make yourself accountable to others, the more likely you are to not only stick to your plan but build upon it.

There are several ways to build accountability into your plan for financial success. You can work with a coach and make commitments to him or her to take specific steps to improve your finances within a defined time frame. For many of the people we work with, weekly meetings with next steps work beautifully to make sure they continue with their progress. Most people are very invested in not disappointing their financial coach, so they take the prescribed steps in between the weekly phone calls, and eventually the progress becomes more habitual. But a coach isn't the only route. Simply sharing your financial goals with people you love and trust, along with setting a time frame to achieve the goals, can provide the accountability you need to deliver on your commitments.

A study on accountability was done by the Association for Talent Development. The researchers found that individuals have the following probabilities of completing a goal by taking these actions:

1. Having an idea or goal: 10 percent likely to complete the goal
2. Consciously deciding that you will do it: 25 percent
3. Deciding when you will do it: 40 percent
4. Planning how to do it: 50 percent
5. Committing to someone that you will do it: 65 percent
6. Having a specific accountability appointment with someone you've committed to: 95 percent[1]

We see this research bear out all the time in real life, so much so that our coaches almost always set "accountability appointments" with employees who are looking to transform their finances quickly. The next story is a case in point.

TYLER'S STORY

Tyler is a 39-year-old HR manager at a large bank. Tyler called Financial Finesse's coaching service in August 2021 because he never had money in the bank and knew that he probably should. He appreciated the guidance the coach gave him, and he had every intent of following it, but then life got in the way—what he now calls "the trifecta." His boyfriend broke up with him, his mother was diagnosed with cancer, and his company went through a merger that required him to spend ridiculously long hours at work trying to help employees acclimate to the new culture.

Then in April 2022 something clicked. His life had settled, and a coworker thanked him for the financial wellness coaching that his HR colleagues responsible for the company's benefits put in place prior to the pandemic. This was the same coaching service he had called right before the trifecta upended his life!

He decided to call again, and the coach, recognizing that he had called in previously but failed to follow up, immediately worked with him to form an accountability plan. Together Tyler and his coach decided each call would include at least one step that Tyler could take to cut expenses and begin saving and investing for his future. After each call, the coach sent Tyler an action plan that included the steps they committed to on the call, along with deadlines to complete each step; they also would set up an appointment where they could go over the results. Each time the coach talked to Tyler, Tyler revealed how he had gone above and beyond what they agreed to because he had a sense of accountability and wanted to exceed both the coach's expectations and his own.

Tyler ultimately went from no savings at all, even proactively opting out of investing in his 401(k), to having a $40,000 emergency fund, saving for a home that he is now in the process of closing on, and maxing out his 401(k). He did this all by progressively cutting expenses for items he didn't really value in the first place and finding low- or no-cost alternatives. Instead he put that money to work toward his future—and he is the first to admit it would have never happened without having his coach as an accountability partner.

Gratification

As humans we are programmed to want instant gratification, especially these days in the era of 10-second TikTok videos. Left alone, this trait can wreak havoc on a solid financial plan, because it is much easier to get instant gratification from consuming than saving. However, you can flip this innately human quality to become an advantage if you find ways to reward yourself for the steps you are taking to make financial progress. We will explore rewards more in the next module, "Tackle Your Financial Stress," but the idea is to celebrate even the smallest successes so you get an immediate sense of gratification when you make a positive change, even before you feel the full impact of that change. In the book *The 100 Simple Secrets of Successful People*, researchers found that perceived self-interest, the rewards one believes are at stake, is the most significant factor in predicting dedication and satisfaction toward work. It accounts for about 75 percent of personal motivation toward accomplishment.[2]

For some people, the best way to get this sense of reward is to keep track of everything they've done. For others, it's using a platform that does this tracking for them and rewards them with an instant improvement in their financial wellness score, as well as recognition of each step they have taken to improve their finances. For still others, it's celebrating victories with their friends or partner. Even telling someone about your progress makes it more rewarding, and certainly having some sort of fun (and ideally low-cost) celebration is an excellent way to get that sense of immediate gratification that we all need to stay on track.

Recovery

Science has confirmed what we all seem to experience every day; it's easier to focus on the negative than the positive. Alison Ledgerwood, behavioral scientist, professor of psychology, and chancellor's fellow at UC Davis, has conducted extensive research to verify and understand this phenomenon and reviews her findings in her TEDxUCDavis talk, "Getting Stuck in the Negatives (and How to Get Unstuck)."[3] This is a hard one for most people. The best advice I have here is to figure out what helps you move from the emotional state we all go through when we have a setback and advance to a rational state without suppressing your natural human emotions (which if you do, will come at you later when you least expect it). You may need to unwind and get your mind off the issue so you are in a better head space when you process it. You may need to talk to a friend, coach, or mentor who can help you put things into perspective. Or like me, you may need some time alone to fully process what happened, feel the sting of the setback, find the lesson, and then regroup more determined than before. To train the mind to focus on the positive, Professor Ledgerwood recommends journaling for just three minutes a day on things you're grateful for. As you dig into identifying your own bright spots, you'll start to figure out how you've successfully bounced back in the past, and you can then make that part of your process.

If you have a hard time with setbacks, one of the best things you can do is find a coach, mentor, or friend who can provide you perspective, so that you don't dwell on your mistake, or worse, let it derail your progress because you feel helpless and decide to quit any efforts to improve your finances. This is exactly the technique that Mark, the subject of our next story, uses.

MARK'S STORY

Mark, 57, is an executive assistant at a consulting firm. Mark calls our Financial Coaching Line when he feels like he made a mistake. Maybe he made a purchase that he regrets; or maybe he invested in something because he was worried about missing out on the action, only later to worry that he has put too much of his hard-earned money at risk; or maybe he did something that he worries will damage his credit score. For Mark, some of these setbacks are actual issues; others are mere worries. But regardless, they feel like problems to him, and in order to gain perspective, he periodically needs a financial coach to listen to him, assess the actual damage that may have occurred, and remind him that "it's going to be OK; this is fixable."

Environment

Your environment—meaning the people you surround yourself with and the situations you put yourself in—is typically a key component of most people's bright spots. There are two essential aspects of setting up your environment that you need to be aware of as you go through the process of identifying your own bright spots: (1) setting up positive influences that support your success and (2) figuring out how to minimize or ideally eliminate the triggers that cause you to backslide.

In terms of positive influences, the most common one we recommend to the people we coach is to automate as much as they can in terms of setting up everything from saving for different financial goals to paying bills. The more you are able to take intentional decision-making out of the process, the less you tax your willpower, which we all have in limited supply. This is why so many people have amassed so much wealth in their company-sponsored retirement plans. Their contributions are automatically deducted from each paycheck. Imagine what would happen if that weren't the case and you had to actually make a deposit after every paycheck into your 401(k)! The vast majority of people would have very little saved simply because they would forget to make the deposit; or they might rationalize a decision not to at a time when they feel they need as large a paycheck as possible to fund their day-to-day expenses.

For items that can't be automated, consider using positive action triggers. Action triggers are basically preloaded decisions made ahead of time to take a certain action when you encounter a certain trigger. For example, if you are striving to save money by taking your lunch to work rather than eating out, an action trigger might be to decide to make your lunch after you hit the brew button on the coffeepot in the morning. A whole body of research in psychology has focused on this phenomenon, finding that the typical person who set an action trigger did better than at least 74 percent of people with the same task who didn't set one.

The second most common recommendation we make to the people we coach is to surround themselves with people who are on the same journey they are on to improve their finances . . . people who encourage and inspire them to make better financial decisions both overtly as part of a support group and more subtly by virtue of how they live. If you pride yourself on being "independent" and doubt that the people in your life impact your success, consider a 2010 study of US Air Force cadets in which researchers tracked a cohort of cadets over four years.[4]

The researchers studied cadets who spent almost all their time interacting with peers in their squadron, which essentially becomes like a second family. Even though all the squadrons trained in exactly the same way, some squadrons showed vast increases in fitness over the four years, whereas others did not. It turns out that the determining factor of whether the 30 cadets within a squadron improved was the motivation of the least-fit person in the group. If the least-fit person was motivated to improve, then his enthusiasm spread and everyone improved. If, on the other hand, the least-fit person was apathetic, or negative, he dragged everyone down.

Bottom line: The more you surround yourself with people who have the habits you aspire to build, the more likely you are to follow their example. Be especially aware of the influence of the "least financially fit" person in your social circle. Getting that person on board with developing better habits not only will transform the person's own finances, but is likely to have a significant impact on your own.

In terms of eliminating negative action triggers—those things that cause you to make decisions you later regret, like spending too much, investing emotionally, or turning control of your finances over to someone else—this is a very personal process. First you have to really pay attention to those things that cause you to fall into old habits—for example, giving in to friends and family who pressure you to spend money, using shopping as a way to feel better after a long day or a hard time, getting caught up in checking your account balance when the market is volatile and impulsively selling investments when they plummet, becoming overwhelmed and letting others make decisions for you that may not be in your best interest, or falling into the trap of buying things you don't need because they are "on sale." Whatever it is, there are ways to mitigate your exposure to situations that trigger you, such as telling your friends and family you are trying to save money and asking that they spend time with you in ways that support your goal, or using your computer during the workday instead of your phone so you aren't bombarded with alerts around what the market is doing.

At this point, you should have everything you need to identify your bright spots and develop a plan for success using the lessons you learn from them. Below are specific action items you can take to accelerate your financial progress with the bright spot concept.

EXERCISE

How You Can Identify Your Own Bright Spots to Accelerate Your Financial Progress

To identify your own bright spots, take these three steps:

1. **Think of at least three accomplishments you made in the face of incredible difficulty, and use the table that follows to identify what you did in each of the key areas that drove your success.** *Please note:* You may not discover patterns in each of these areas, and that's OK. They are there to help you organize and potentially expand your thinking, but "more" is not the goal here. The goal is to uncover your most powerful bright spots so you can use them to amplify your success going forward. For most people, this is three to five key things—more than that can become overwhelming.

	Accomplishment 1	Accomplishment 2	Accomplishment 3
What did you do to keep yourself motivated?			
How did you hold yourself accountable in order to avoid temptation to abandon your plan?			
How did you reward yourself for the progress you made?			
What did you do to recover from setbacks?			
How did you set your environment up to support your success?			
What did you do to remove triggers?			

2. **Now look at what you've written down. What are the patterns you see that have driven your successes?** These patterns are the bright spots you can tap into in order to accelerate your financial progress.

3. **Now make a plan to put your bright spots to work so you can begin to reap the financial benefits.** Identify the most important financial challenges you are facing or difficult goals you want to achieve, and determine how you can use the bright spots you identified above to set yourself up for success.

Module 2

TACKLE YOUR FINANCIAL STRESS

ABOUT THIS MODULE

Now that you've set yourself up for financial success, you will be in a great position to reduce and ideally eliminate your financial stress. Doing so is critical to having the bandwidth to focus on long-term financial goals.

This module is designed to supplement your plan for setting yourself up for financial success by reducing the financial stress that is holding you back. You may think financial stress is more of a mental health challenge—that it doesn't in and of itself affect your finances. But the reality couldn't be further from the truth. As you'll learn going through this module, financial stress is not only mentally taxing, but physically taxing—negatively impacting everything from chronic health conditions to your ability to make good long-term decisions. It also has a downward spiral effect on your financial life—lowering your productivity and ability to focus at work; putting your relationships, most commonly your marriage, in jeopardy (financial challenges are a leading cause of divorce); and putting your brain in a state of constant "fight or flight," which compromises your ability to think beyond the immediate issue at hand. You simply cannot achieve the life you want until you free yourself of the feeling of financial stress and address the core issues that are causing your stress.

This module is your guide to doing both, as well as bulletproofing your finances so that you ensure financial stress is a thing of the past.

But there's one caveat, and that is for people facing a financial crisis: If you are facing a financial crisis, where you are close to losing your home or having trouble providing the basic necessities for your family, you don't have the time to go through the steps outlined in this module. You must take immediate action. If this is your situation, *skip directly to Chapter 9* to get the help you need. Once you resolve your financial crisis, you can always revisit this module. In our financial coaching, we find that once people resolve a financial crisis, they are incredibly motivated to ensure that they take whatever steps are needed to avoid ending up in a similar situation down the road. These people are among the most successful at permanently reducing their financial stress and getting to a place where they are able to intention-ally plan and achieve important financial goals. So if this is your situation, know that the guidance will be there once you have your crisis resolved; and at that point, you'll actually be in the ideal state of mind to permanently overcome your financial stress.

5

GET IMMEDIATE RELIEF FROM YOUR FINANCIAL STRESS

S tress is a combination of our anxiety level and the seriousness of the problem causing the anxiety. As humans, all of us are subject to feeling stress and anxiety. But as individuals, we each have our own inherent sensitivity to anxiety and stress. Some people can go through a terribly traumatic event with relatively minimal stress, simply because of the way their brain is wired. Others like me can experience a minor setback and respond with high levels of stress. Most people are somewhere in the middle, with specific situations that trigger a high level of stress based on past traumas and other situations that they are able to glide gracefully through because they automatically process the situation as temporary and solvable.

It took me years to realize that we all have an "anxiety set point"— a natural anxiety level that is hardwired into our personality. You can't change this; it's simply part of who you are, and you'll actually become more stressed if you try to change it. What you can do, though, is (1) acknowledge it and (2) manage it.

SO HOW DO YOU MANAGE
YOUR FINANCIAL STRESS?

Managing your financial stress is actually harder than managing most other stressors. Most stressors are temporary in nature—from day-to-day aggravations like delayed flights and long waits in traffic, to the dreaded visit to the dentist, to frustrating work meetings or projects, to conflict with friends and loved ones that feels stressful at the time, but like a distant memory days later. Situational stress can be rough in the moment, but typically it passes quickly.

Financial stress, on the other hand, tends to last until the situation causing it is resolved, and as we know, changing your financial situation takes time. So all the stress hormones—most notably cortisol, the flight-or-fight hormone I referred to in the introduction—course through your body for a much longer time and end up taxing your mental and physical health, your relationships, and your performance at work. Obviously, resolving the financial issues causing the stress will make the biggest impact on your quality of life, but there are things you can do before you reach that point to manage your stress so it doesn't harm your well-being.

Below are the most effective stress reduction techniques our coaches use with clients who call us in a state of high stress and are undergoing major financial challenges that will take time to resolve.

1. Understand you are *not* alone.

When we go through hard times, we tend to feel very isolated and even ashamed. We often don't want to share our problems with others, for fear that they will judge us or be disappointed with us or that we will "burden" them. So we suffer in silence, and the stress grows because we shoulder it all alone, without tapping into a support system that can provide us with a sense of release and perspective. When we try to deal with our stresses on our own, they compound rather than diminish, as do the feelings of isolation and shame, which in turn make us even more resistant to discussing the situation with anyone else. Eventually it starts to feel like we have a "dirty little secret," and the stress of feeling like we are hiding something important becomes unbearable.

You don't have to live this way. Studies show that simply by sharing what is stressing you out with someone you trust, who not only can listen but can be a sounding board when you are ready to discuss resolutions, cortisol levels are reduced, and stress levels are significantly lowered.[1]

The benefits of a single conversation can last days in terms of stress relief—probably why weekly visits to a therapist have become the standard for those dealing with stress and anxiety.

In fact, my team and I continually monitor the responses of surveys sent following financial coaching sessions, and one of the most common comments we receive on the surveys is that the coaching session itself relieved the respondent's stress—even though the person hadn't yet implemented the steps discussed with the coach.

The good news is that you don't need a financial coach or therapist in this case to reap the full benefits! If you need a sympathetic ear and wise counsel, you can go to anyone you trust who has your best interests at heart and won't judge you.

Just beware, if you do go to a friend or mentor as opposed to a financial coach with formal training and experience in the field of financial counseling and planning, you should have a very candid conversation about the person's financial expertise—where the person can help you and where he or she doesn't have the knowledge or experience to do so. The last thing you want is a well-intentioned mentor giving you guidance that isn't financially sound and ultimately puts you in a worse financial position.

2. As part of understanding you are not alone, know that whatever you are going through, there are millions of others who have gone through similar challenges and have not only overcome their issues but achieved financial security.

It is natural to feel like what you are facing is somehow much worse than what others have gone through. It's that Instagram lifestyle phenomenon that makes us think that everyone else is so much better off than we are, that we somehow are uniquely defective in a world where everyone else has everything figured out. In reality this couldn't be further from the truth! Our financial coaches talk to people every single day who are overwhelmed with financial stress and beating themselves up for being so far behind their peers. The truth is that the vast majority of people feel this way, so you are not the outlier at all! What you are going through, for better or worse, is incredibly common . . . so much so that our financial coaches consider it to be a part of the financial journey that comes with being human! The reality of living in a world where you have finite money and infinite choices around how to spend, save, and invest that money (as well as how to lose it if you aren't careful!) naturally sets you up for stress. Compound that with the fact that no one *really* prepares us for how to manage our finances as an adult, and we have a perfect storm that makes financial challenges and the ensuing financial stress practically inevitable—*unless we take the steps necessary to intentionally manage both.*

3. Let go of shame and fully accept that you *cannot* change the past, so there's no reason to spend more time regretting what you did or didn't do.

Nor is there reason to spend time lamenting the things that happened completely outside your control that put you in your current situation. I remind myself of this every single day. Life is finite, and we have two choices—spend the time we have left on creating the best future possible or spend it ruminating over a past we can never change. When you catch yourself obsessing over your past, remind yourself of that. Shaping your future is incredibly energizing and impactful—and will result in you doing everything you can to build the life you want. Every minute you take away from that by punishing yourself for your past is not just a waste of time; it's taking away from the future you are trying to build for yourself and your loved ones.

JOE'S STORY
Shame had created a stack of mail on Joe's counter. Joe, a retail employee in his late twenties, found himself in a situation that scared him too much to look at. He had been mismanaging his cash flow, which led him

to depend on payday loans to get him from one paycheck to the next. In order to maximize his take-home pay to try to catch up with the payday loans, he stopped contributing to his 401(k), and he had been "advised" by a friend to increase his federal tax withholdings to 99, resulting essentially in withholding nothing for federal taxes from his paycheck. Joe is a smart man, and he knew that he would have to pay in when he filed his taxes. So he decided to not file his taxes . . . for seven years. He happened to mention this casually to his mentor, who told him to get help immediately in order to avoid severe consequences.

Joe called our coaching line deeply ashamed to share his story, terrified of being judged or, as he told his coach later, "turned in to the IRS." It took two hours of coaching, but he was finally able to share his reality with someone besides his mentor—the secret he had been harboring for years. And when he did, he immediately felt better—like a weight had been lifted. The coach had seen situations worse than his and didn't judge his past actions. Instead the coach focused Joe on looking at his situation objectively so he could stop blaming himself for what he called "the mess he created" and move forward to fix it. Joe bravely contacted the IRS and developed a plan to pay his back taxes, and then worked with his coach to make changes in his spending so he could pay off not only his taxes, but all his other debts. He is now in a relationship with a woman he would never have had the confidence to pursue in the past because of the shame he felt over his finances, and they are planning on getting married and buying a home together—all things he never would have thought remotely possible before he finally let go of his shame and worked through how to move forward.

4. Remind yourself that *nothing* in life is permanent.

Your financial situation changes *every single day*, and when you look over the course of most people's lives, there's typically a huge difference from where they start financially and where they end up. In the field of stress management, there's a technique many therapists use to help people under stress achieve a healthy perspective. This is to think about how you are going to feel about the situation you are in over the next five days, five weeks, five months, and five years. Chances are that, over time, you won't even remember the details of your current financial situation because you'll be in such a different place. You may remember the stress, but even that will probably feel more like a life lesson than a deeply traumatic time. You will have forgotten what life used to be like when financial stress was omnipresent because you'll have reached a high enough level of financial freedom and security that it's hard to imagine there was ever a time that this security was not a part of your daily life.

5. Actively pay attention to the level of stress you feel at any given moment, and be aware of what works best for you to reduce this stress.

For me, it's talking things through with someone I trust and feeling like I have a path forward to reduce the stress. I also benefit from reading inspirational stories of others who have gone through similar challenges and prevailed, or even better, talking to people who have overcome whatever I am going through and serve as validation that I, too, can and will prevail.

For some, it may be deep breathing or meditation, or it may be physical exercise to get their stressful energy out of their system and replace it with endorphins that provide a sense of peace.

For others, it may be getting away from their hectic day-to-day lives. For example, nature is especially calming and naturally brings perspective, so taking a break from it all to go on a walk or hike will reduce stress, as will simply enjoying a beautiful setting that reminds you there's a whole world outside of what you are going through and anchors you to a sense of something larger than yourself that existed long before you did and will continue to exist long after.

Still others find peace in religion, church, and prayer and the support network that comes with belonging to a community of like-minded people that they trust.

The important thing is to figure out what techniques work best for you and to turn to them when your stress starts to peak. Over time, you'll find that you are able to effectively manage your stress, so that it isn't as heavy and omnipresent as it was and doesn't drag you down physically, mentally, and emotionally.

Sometimes managing your stress can directly lead to extra income! Take Tina's story as an example.

TINA'S STORY

Tina, a 47-year-old mother of two teenagers who presented their own set of challenges, worked in a high-stress job as a call center manager for an insurance company. To manage the stress of home and work, she used Pilates as active therapy, but her budget was really tight. Her financial coach suggested that teaching Pilates would keep it incorporated in her life and could also bring in a little extra cash. Tina reached out to the people who ran her local Pilates studio to propose becoming one of the instructors, and they were thrilled to have her.

6. Make a plan.

Stress and anxiety are largely rooted in feeling "out of control" and, at extreme levels, even hopeless. One of the best ways to rid yourself of that feeling is to create a plan, both to improve your finances and to reduce your stress. (See the exercise at the end of the chapter, which lays out the steps you can take to create a personal stress reduction plan.) From a financial perspective, your situation may not be immediately resolvable, but you can at least take action to begin improving it. I share more in Chapter 6 about plans you can put in place to overcome different financial challenges, but the key to success here is universal: (1) You want a plan that is realistic, meaning you can stick to it. (2) You want a plan that is trackable, so that you can see your progress and feel a sense of both accomplishment and relief, which will keep you motivated to continue the plan. And (3) you want a plan that is automated where possible, so you don't have to think about it. Where you can't automate, it should be fully integrated into your life in the form of habits and routines that become part of how you live your life.

It's tempting to want to resolve your financial challenges really quickly in order to get immediate relief from financial stress. But the reality is that you have to be kind and patient with yourself so you can develop a plan you can realistically stick to instead of trying to make too many changes and failing because it simply is too hard to sustain.

7. Celebrate the steps you are taking to improve your situation as important successes—even if you haven't yet fully resolved the financial challenges you are facing.

The reality is that it takes time to improve your finances. So if you are anchoring how you feel about yourself and your money to successfully eliminating all your debt, building a large savings account, or achieving major financial goals, you are setting yourself up to feel stressed until you actually reach these milestones; and that may take anywhere from months to many years—far too long to be under high or overwhelming financial stress. Instead give yourself credit for taking the steps to improve your finances. You can do this in one of two ways:

1. By breaking your plan into steps—essentially making a to-do list—and rewarding yourself once you cross an item off the list. For example, suppose you find a way to cut $3 a day in expenses and have taken that $90 per month to pay off your highest interest rate card through setting up an automatic payment plan; if so, you've likely put yourself in a position to save thousands (possibly tens of thousands) in interest over time and cut the time it will take you to get out of debt by a decade or more. That's huge! You shouldn't wait to celebrate this accomplishment until you are out of debt; instead celebrate the *actions* you are taking that will get you there faster and save you thousands in the process.

2. By using a tool that tracks your progress based on actions you are taking instead of simply tracking your current financial situation. This is best done through a digital financial wellness assessment available online or as an app, as part of your financial well-being benefits at work. A good financial wellness assessment is typically provided by an independent financial coaching

firm that doesn't sell financial products or services and is comprehensive enough to give you a true picture of your overall financial wellness, factoring in the current actions you are taking to improve your financial wellness. The process should last about five to eight minutes and should cover a broad range of questions around what you are doing to manage your finances. Your score will reflect these actions, so you'll be able to see immediate improvement as you take the steps vital to achieving financial stability, such as cutting expenses to live within your means, paying more than the minimums on your high interest rate debt, beginning to fund an emergency savings account, and working to improve your credit. You'll be able to see your score increase as you begin taking these steps, and further increase as you make progress completing them, so you won't have to wait for that sense of gratification and accomplishment and will have the motivation to continue your progress.

FINANCIAL WELLNESS ASSESSMENT EXAMPLE

Ask your employer if an assessment like the one shown in Figure 5.1 is available to you.

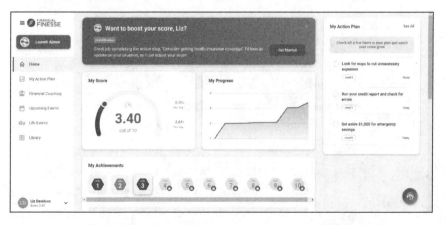

FIGURE 5.1   Financial Wellness Assessment example

EXERCISE

Build Your Own Stress Reduction Plan

The above techniques have been scientifically proven to reduce stress, but they are broad recommendations, not personalized ones. To best manage your own stress, you have to develop a stress reduction plan that is designed around what works best for you. Here's how to do that:

Step 1. Think about the times you've successfully gotten through stressful situations and what you did to manage your stress during those times. Write down the things that helped the most.

Step 2. Think of the unhealthy ways you cope with stress (we all have them) that aren't serving you, and replace them with better habits. Here are some examples:

- **Go-to coping mechanism.** Drinking heavily at the end of a hard day to "take the edge off" (my initial impulse during stressful days during the pandemic).
- **Replacement habit.** Doing something you love that relieves stress—for me, that was dancing, earbuds in blaring mostly 1970s dance tunes. I started off joyous because dancing brings me an immediate release of pure bliss, and finished when I was exhausted but full of endorphins. Afterward the thought of having a drink turned my stomach, and before I knew it, the dancing became a habit.
- **Go-to coping mechanism.** Shopping to get a feel-good rush.
- **Replacement habit.** Doing something else that gives you that feel-good rush—something that fills your soul without draining your bank account. This could be anything from engaging in creative projects, to volunteering, to pursuing a hobby that you love.

- **Go-to coping mechanism.** Falling prey to quick-fix solutions that appear to provide an immediate way out of your situation but actually can set you further behind. These include taking out payday loans, buying into "get-rich-quick" ventures promising significant monthly income but usually requiring some sort of down payment to get started, and changing jobs impulsively for a signing bonus or higher salary only to discover the total benefits package and/or the work expected of you actually sets you further behind in the long run, financially and from a fulfillment standpoint.
- **Replacement habit.** Find an accountability partner—a good friend, mentor, or coach—whom you can call when you get tempted to make decisions that provide short-term relief but are not in your best interest long term.

Step 3. Create a plan based on the above as well as the suggestions in this module that you feel will be the most helpful to you. Pick one to three things you are going to do on a daily or weekly basis to reduce your stress, and pick one to three new stress reduction habits that you are going to use to replace habits that are not serving your well-being and may even be sabotaging it. Set time in your calendar for the things you have chosen, and hold that time sacred the same way you would an important business meeting or family event. It's easy to say, "I'm too busy to do that!" but the reality is that if you don't invest this time in yourself, you will ultimately be less productive and less able to bring your best self to all the things, big and small, you need to do to succeed at work, to foster the best relationships with your loved ones, and ultimately to build a fulfilling life.

6

OVERCOMING YOUR FINANCIAL CHALLENGES

O nce you have a plan to manage your financial stress, the next step is to get to the root cause of the stress so you don't have stress you need to manage! This chapter takes you through the different financial circumstances that cause financial stress, with guidance on how to tackle each one so you can move forward financially without being weighed down with anxiety.

To do this, you have to first understand where you are financially, because that will help you determine the root cause of your stress and how best to tackle it. There are four categories that people fall into when it comes to their overall situation, and each has its unique set of stressors. Here are brief descriptions of the categories so you can identify where you are financially:

■ **Suffering.** People in this category are going through a financial crisis. They are struggling to meet basic needs and close to losing their housing, or they are at a point where they are making compromises that jeopardize the safety and well-being of themselves or their loved ones.

- **Struggling.** People in this category are not facing a financial crisis, but they may be living paycheck to paycheck and using credit cards to fund shortfalls. They are struggling to create positive cash flow that can be used to pay down debt and save for emergencies.
- **Planning.** People in this category have a solid financial foundation in terms of making ends meet, managing debt, and having a savings account to tap into in case of emergencies. Still, they are struggling to either plan for or achieve key financial goals and feeling anxiety from being "behind" their peers or their own vision they set for themselves.
- **Optimizing.** People in this category have achieved a high level of financial security but may be worried about losing it due to a declining stock market or other economic conditions that threaten to drain the wealth they've worked so hard to build.

Now that you've identified where you fit, skip to the corresponding section below that is most relevant to you.

SUFFERING

If you are in the suffering category, that means you are facing a financial crisis right now that you must resolve to ensure you keep your housing and have sufficient money to provide for basic needs for yourself and your family. The good news is that temporary support may be available through your employer, community, and government resources; and depending on the state you live in, there may be laws that give you protection against eviction if you are facing financial hardship. The bad news is that a financial crisis is serious and needs to be addressed immediately so you can stay in your housing and are able to support your basic needs.

NOTE

If this is your situation, *please skip immediately to Chapter 9* for resources you can tap to resolve your financial crisis.

STRUGGLING

According to our research, which includes analyzing the financial wellness assessments of over 517,000 employed Americans, 65 percent of US employees fit into the financially struggling category at any one time, meaning they are barely making ends meet and are at risk of not being able to weather a financial emergency. And that is just looking at a single point in time. The number is much higher when you consider how many people fall into the struggling category at some point in their life. Some people struggle at the beginning of their careers when they are making entry-level salaries and dealing with student loan payments coupled with all the challenges that come with supporting yourself financially for the first time. For others, financial struggle is a result of a setback like divorce, disability, or the death of a spouse or partner that compromises your ability to continue to fund your current lifestyle. And then there are those who are simply dealing with juggling multiple priorities in life and struggling to make ends meet as a result.

So how do you know if you fit into the struggling category when it comes to your finances? People who are struggling financially feel that they are constantly one step away from a financial crisis, and that they are barely hanging on in the days right before getting their paycheck. Many people that are struggling have to time purchases around payday, or they have to resort to purchasing on credit because they don't have the money in the bank to pay their expenses in full. They also may find that they are making compromises they aren't happy about for financial reasons—such as taking on extra hours at a job that they don't like or that takes them away from their families, or compromising on daycare or education for their children because they simply can't afford the kind of facility or school they feel would best serve their children's needs.

If it sounds like you, know that most other people are in the same boat—so what you might think as shameful or representative of you "not keeping up" with others you see living their "best lives," that reality couldn't be further from the truth. That doesn't mean you shouldn't try to fix the situation—as it is incredibly stressful and obviously keeps you from having the freedom you need to live the life you want. It just means that it's a natural human phenomenon to have trouble managing money in a way that grows wealth. A 2022 study found that 36 percent of those making $250,000 or more report having trouble making ends meet.[1]

The reality is that humans are set up to struggle unless they take conscious steps not to, simply because money is a limited resource in a world of unlimited choices around how to spend it. Absent intentionally taking the steps to set yourself up for success and then putting a concrete plan in place to improve your financial situation, you are likely to spend more than you make, fund the difference with debt, and fall further behind over time. There are simply too many opportunities to go down this path—increasing your consumption at a faster rate than your pay as you see others do the same. And that's not taking into account those who have more modest financial resources to work with in the first place. In these cases, it is naturally harder to get out of the struggling spiral and start saving, and usually takes ongoing financial coaching to not only make a plan, but ensure you are sticking to it—an accountability partner who can be there for you when things get really hard.

HOW TO MOVE FROM FINANCIALLY STRUGGLING TO FINANCIAL STABILITY

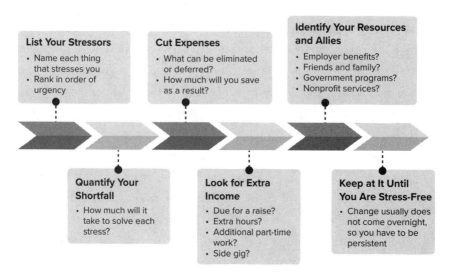

FIGURE 6.1 The path to financial stability

Figure 6.1 summarizes many of the key points we will be discussing in this chapter to give you a visual representation of how you can go about overcoming the financial challenges that are causing you financial stress and holding you back from progressing toward your most important financial goals. However, it's important to keep in mind that not everyone's situation fits into a nice, neat little box where they can follow the steps outlined in the previous figure to solve their problems. Some people don't have room to cut expenses; others don't have time to work a second job; still others may lack support from family or friends. The reality is that you need to create a plan that works for you, based on your situation.

This starts with getting honest about the core issues that are causing the struggle in the first place, and determining which solutions are going to work best for you to address those issues so you can progress financially.

Here are the most common core issues, along with guidance on how to resolve them:

1. Debt

Debt is the most common reason that most people are struggling, because the amount of interest they are paying puts them in the red each month. This creates a snowball effect, where they have to put more on their credit cards to pay their bills, thus incurring more debt, which means more interest payments. And the cycle continues.

If debt is your core issue, there are two key areas to focus on:

- First and foremost, eliminating your high interest rate debt—this is the most efficient way to get relief from burdensome interest payments.
- Separately, you'll want to look at potentially reducing your overall debt level—because even low interest rate debt can become a problem if you are struggling to keep up with the total monthly interest payments. A common rule of thumb is to keep your total debt payments within 36 percent of your gross monthly income. This includes your mortgage payment as well as any other debt.

Most people we coach are pleasantly surprised that they can significantly reduce their debt by making relatively minor changes to their spending habits that don't compromise their quality of life and simply directing that extra money toward their debt, focusing on their highest interest rate debt first to pay down their debt as quickly as possible. For others, the solution may require more creativity—including making more significant expense cuts and finding ways to generate extra income—but they are still able to prevail.

However, we do sometimes work with people who are drowning in debt—and have already tried reducing expenses, bringing in more income, and even negotiating with their creditors. In these cases, we recommend these people pursue other options. If this is your situation, here's a step-by-step guide to follow:

STEP 1. LOOK INTO CREDIT COUNSELING

Credit counseling is a process of reviewing your credit report and budget and then offering a personalized plan to help you find relief from financial pressure. It's provided by trained and certified financial counselors for little or no cost when you use an agency affiliated with nonprofit organizations like the National Foundation for Credit Counseling (NFCC). If the plan your credit counseling agency creates is something that you feel you can implement without further help, then this is the best route for you.

STEP 2. IF CREDIT COUNSELING ISN'T ENOUGH,
THEN LOOK AT GETTING A DEBT MANAGEMENT PLAN

Some people need more help because their level of debt is too high to resolve through debt consolidation and cutting expenses. If this is the case for you, then the best next step is to consider a debt management plan. This plan involves credit counselors helping you set up agreements with your various creditors, which may include getting fees waived and interest rates lowered. Most legitimate credit counseling agencies will charge you a small monthly fee for this service.

Beware of any credit counseling agencies that require you to pay them a lump sum up front, or say they will work for free and simply take a "cut" of the money they save you. At best, these agencies are overcharging you; at worst they may be fraudulent.

By far, the best model is to pay the monthly fee, and have the agency negotiate with your creditors on your behalf.

STEP 3. AS A LAST RESORT, CONSIDER BANKRUPTCY

A legitimate credit counseling agency (like those affiliated with the NFCC) will be very honest with you about your situation and will let you know if a debt management plan isn't going to be sufficient to resolve your debt problems. Legitimate agencies know from experience how much impact they can make negotiating down your debt, and if they believe that your debt levels are so high that even their best negotiating efforts won't solve the problem, they will tell you. At this point, it is time to consider bankruptcy. The good news here is that by starting with credit counseling, you'll already have completed the first step that is usually required when filing for personal bankruptcy. If you just jump straight to engaging a bankruptcy firm, typically the firm will charge you for this step. Since in most cases, you can get that service for little or no cost through organizations like the NFCC, be sure to check into that before paying for a bankruptcy counseling service.

2. Lifestyle Expenses

The vast majority of people we work with are spending money on things they don't even care much about, often at the expense of their financial health and sanity. The reality is that as little as a few dollars a day can make a huge difference in both reducing debt and establishing an emergency savings account, and most people are able to find this money by doing small things like cutting subscription services they aren't using, carpooling or taking public transportation instead of driving to reduce the cost of gas, entertaining friends at home more often and dining out less, and taking advantage of employee benefits to pay for things they would otherwise pay for out of pocket. These are just a few examples; our coaches have uncovered thousands of ways employees can cut expenses without compromising their quality of life, and instead use that money to pay off debts, save for emergencies, and begin working toward key financial goals.

To quote one of our financial coaches on a recent Financial Finesse podcast, paying off $27,000 in debt happens $8 at a time. This was in reference to Mary, a woman he coached who got out of $27,000 in debt within a single year by simply making different choices about how she spent her money.

MARY'S STORY

Mary followed the framework we provide people interested in reducing their debt:

First, Mary worked with her financial coach to identify expenses that she could cut that would actually improve her quality of life—things like not dining out on junk food as much and instead preparing healthier meals at home; not going to the mall to get her shopping "fix" after a hard day of work and instead exercising out her frustration; and teaching her children fiscal responsibility by providing them with an allowance rather than buying them what they wanted in real time, at the store, when she was exhausted already and didn't want yet another argument.

Second, she changed her mindset about money to better align her spending with the things she really valued. She realized that she was spending money on things that she didn't care about to impress others. As a result, she traded in her nice car for a less glamorous but safer form of transportation, and she returned to her love of nature, taking her kids hiking and camping in lieu of more luxurious vacations where they would spend their time mostly indoors on their electronic devices regardless!

Between consolidating her debt to a much lower interest rate credit card and using the savings from cutting these expenses to increase her debt payments, she was completely free of all high interest rate debt in less than a year, with her low interest rate mortgage as the only outstanding debt she had.

EXERCISE

Determine what expenses you can cut—expenses that might feel good in the moment but don't serve you in the long term and may even be hurting your health, well-being, or self-esteem. Examples:

- Shopping to feel better instead of doing things that improve your well-being (exercising, time with friends)
- Expensive car payments when a less expensive car would be a better option
- Dining out versus making healthier meals at home
- Succumbing to a child's requests when shopping
- Choosing paid activities versus free ones (nature hikes)

If you reduced or eliminated these expenses, how much could you save each month?

What would happen if you took the money you saved and directed it to the highest interest rate debt? Use the tool shown in Figure 6.2; it's available for you to access at www.ffcalcs.com/debt_blaster.

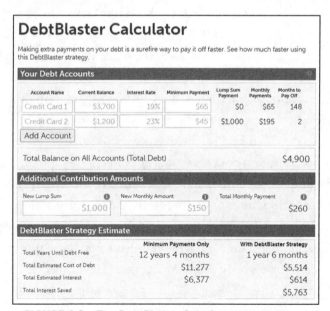

FIGURE 6.2 The DebtBlaster Calculator was designed to help you reduce or eliminate your debt.

3. Fixed or Necessary Expenses That Are Too High

This is a tough one to reckon with for most people, because reducing fixed or necessary expenses—especially when it comes to your rent or mortgage—can mean changing your lifestyle or quality of life, at least for a period of time until you are able to pay off debts, generate more income, or find clever ways to reduce other expenses over time. The good news is that there are creative ways to reduce necessary expenses. In some cases, you can even increase your quality of life at the same time. Here are some examples:

■ **Rent or mortgage.** You can downsize or move to an area of the country where the cost of real estate (as well as the cost of living) is considerably lower. Now that many more companies offer employees the option to work remotely, it has become much easier to relocate without having to risk losing your job. This is obviously easiest if you are single and hardest if you are relocating a large family, but it is an option that can make a huge difference. There are even communities that are actively seeking remote workers and are willing to provide grants to people who move to their towns! By relocating, especially if you get a grant from a community you'd like to live in, you will likely save a significant amount of money and get a more spacious house at the same time! Check real estate values in different areas of the country on the Interactive Median Home Price Map provided by *Realtor Magazine*.[2]

■ **Transportation cost (everything from car payments, maintenance, and gas to other forms of transportation like ridesharing, train or air travel, etc.).** Most people have room to make significant cuts here by taking the following steps: (1) reevaluating their car payment or lease and determining if it makes sense to buy or lease a car that is less expensive and/or that gets better mileage, (2) walking or riding a bike/scooter instead of driving if you live in a safe area and are spending a lot of time making relatively short trips—excellent for your physical and mental health and the environment, (3) carpooling with friends where possible to save on gas and car maintenance expenses, (4) making sure you are getting reimbursed for all work-related travel expenses per your company policy, and (5) using low-cost or free public transport where it is safe and efficient instead of driving or using a rideshare service.

- **Food.** Food is obviously a necessity, but dining out is not. Look at the combination of your grocery bill and the money you spend dining out, and determine what you can do to cut without compromising the quality and healthiness of your diet. Ideally, try to find ways to both reduce costs and eat healthier at the same time by making home-cooked meals, leveraging leftovers (which often taste better the next day anyway), entertaining friends at home instead of dining out, and doing things like couponing, which can be especially fun if you are a bargain hunter.

EXERCISE

The best guidance I have here is to take a look at all the necessary expenses you have simply to live your life so you know what you are working with and can see where there are opportunities to make changes.

Here's a list to get you started:

- Mortgage or rent (ideally should be no more than 28 percent of your income, with the understanding that certain areas are more costly because they offer safer housing, in which case limit as much as you can but focus on cutting other expenses)
- Utilities
- Transportation expenses
- Cell phone, Wi-Fi, and cable expenses
- Unreimbursed work expenses
- Food

- Childcare expenses (if applicable)
- Petcare expenses (if applicable)

Once you identify your necessary expenses, rank them in order of priority, and write down how much you are spending. Then determine what changes you can make to reduce each expense, with a focus on the highest-priority items.

---

4. Not Enough Dollars Coming In

Fortunately, most people can ultimately reach financial stability without needing to increase their income, but there are cases where increasing your income is the best solution; this is especially true for low-income employees who have limited resources to cover all their expenses.

If you have gone through the budgeting process and reduced all the expenses you reasonably can, then your issue is most likely not about what you are spending but how much income you are making. In this case, the solution is to find a way to generate more income, whether taking on additional work, determining what you need to do to secure a pay increase, or creating a side hustle that will get you in a position where you actually have extra money at the end of the month to save and invest in your future. Over time, we find that most people are able to progress to a point that their primary career provides sufficient income, especially if they are working for an employer who has a strong career training and development program in place and a history of promoting employees from within. Others discover that they make more money being "self-employed" and are happier with the flexibility that provides. And then there are those entrepreneurial success stories that emerge from people who started a small business on the side to supplement their income, only to discover that they end up making more from their side business than from their actual job. So if this is your situation, there will be some sacrifices you have to make, but most likely they will be temporary, and you'll end up with a more permanent solution to the lack of income that doesn't necessitate you working overtime to make ends meet.

Our next story is a tale of what is possible when you go through serious financial stress and is proof positive you can progressively work through your financial challenges to get to a better place.

MELISSA'S STORY

Melissa's story serves as an inspiration to anyone facing overwhelming financial stress, where things feel completely helpless, and it's hard to even imagine achieving any sort of relief, let alone building a deeply fulfilling, purposeful life.

Melissa, 55, was married for over 25 years. During that time, she and her husband raised five children, in a highly affluent community. She truly had the "Instagram life" most people covet, including what she called the "best job ever" as a part-time consultant for a firm that helped nonprofits with fund-raising—something that extended to her personal life where she regularly hosted large black-tie events to fund-raise for the causes she believed in. As is the case in many households, her husband, a CEO of a company he started, managed the finances, with Melissa trusting him implicitly and never learning the details of their actual financial situation. It turns out that his company wasn't doing well at all, and he had borrowed against basically everything meaningful they owned, in an effort to sustain his company, and without telling her. The betrayal, coupled with the fact that she found out he was having an affair with his cofounder, was too much for her to bear.

They divorced in 2018, and following the divorce, she saw no other alternative than to file for bankruptcy. Melissa lost her home due to her husband's recklessness and couldn't even afford a very small place of her own. Luckily, she wasn't forced into being truly homeless. She lived with her youngest son and his family for over three years. During that time, she worked with both a counselor she found through her company's employee assistance program and one of our financial coaches to go through the entire process of managing her stress and coming to acceptance of the situation. In both cases, these resources were free to her as a fully subsidized employee benefit—a huge win given the fact she was trying to save every cent she could.

It was rough at first—she was alternatively devastated, furious, hopeless, and overwhelmed by the thought of all the work she would have to do to recover both financially and emotionally. For a full year after everything happened, she wasn't convinced she would ever recover, at least not fully. But through time, and the support of her therapist, coach, and loved ones who were her greatest champions, she came to realize that while she would never live the lifestyle she previously enjoyed, she could create a new life that was more meaningful based on her most important values, which were to spend time with her family and to do what she could to help those less fortunate than her. Even with all her setbacks, she recognized she was lucky to have a place to live with a son and grandson she loved, and a job (which she now worked at in full-time capacity) that gave her a deep sense of fulfillment.

As she let go of the past and began to plan for her own financial future, she became a force to be reckoned with. She secured a promotion at her job, boosting her income significantly. She also decided to take on a second job tutoring children in reading and math at a local tutoring center—using that teaching certification that she received shortly after she got married. Between that and the money she saved by living with her son, she was able to accumulate enough for her to ultimately achieve three key milestones that turned her finances around:

1. She worked with her financial coach to improve her credit, which had been decimated after her husband had stopped paying their joint debts. It took time. To start a new credit history, she had to start out using a secure credit card backed by what she had in the bank. She was also able to dispute many of the debts her now ex-husband had incurred that she hadn't known about and get them taken off her credit report. Slowly but surely, as she established a track record for paying her credit card off on time, her credit score began to improve to a point where she could rent an apartment of her own, which she was able to afford thanks to the income she brought in from her two jobs and the money she was able to save by staying with her son.

2. She was able to build up significant savings in the three years she lived with her son. In time, she got to the point where she not only had enough for a deposit on an apartment, but had a fully funded emergency savings fund and a company-sponsored retirement plan that was rapidly growing. In fact, she was able to max out her retirement contributions and take advantage of the "catch-up contribution," which allowed her to invest more because she was over 50. The upshot was that for each of the three years she lived with her son, she was able to invest over $25,000 per year in her 401(k) plan, with plans to continue contributing the maximum until she ultimately retired.

3. Over time, she was able to leave her apartment, buy a home, and begin building equity.

Today, between her home equity, 401(k) plan, and estimated Social Security payments, she is ironically on track to retire at the age she originally planned before all this happened—at age 65—though she's enjoying both her jobs so much, she's not sure she wants to! Along the way, as she rebuilt her life from the ground up, something significant happened—she discovered she was actually happier without her husband and all the trappings of the life he once provided. Her life had a greater sense of purpose, and her children enjoyed getting to know their mom as an individual. Also, both the friendships she kept from her old life (most left her after the bankruptcy) and the friendships she has developed since then were, in her words, "much more real."

Melissa has told her coach that most people look at her situation and feel sorry for her. Her reply—"Don't. Outside of having my children, it's the best thing that ever happened to me."

EXERCISE

Reduce or eliminate the gap between what you are making and what you need to make to cover your expenses. Here's how you can do it:

- Make a short plan to close that gap, using the following ideas as a starting point:
  - Work more hours at your current job (provided you are paid hourly).
  - Take on an additional job.
  - Start a side hustle.
- Make a long-term plan so you don't have to work unnecessarily hard just to pay the bills, using the following ideas as a starting point:
  - Determine what you can do to grow your career so you can get a raise or promotion (or better yet, a series of them over time).
  - Ask your employer what career development or training resources the company has available to help you build your skills and increase your value.
  - If you discover your side hustle is taking off and starting to bring in enough money to close the gap, consider becoming self-employed. Just remember, you'll need to make about 30 to 40 percent more to cover the loss of your employer's benefits, and you'll need to make sure you set up a plan to pay taxes since you won't be getting taxes taken out of your paycheck anymore.

Financial Stress When You Aren't Struggling

Financial stress is not limited to those who are struggling financially. Remember what I said earlier about stress being the combination of our mindset (including our natural level of anxiety) about a situation and the underlying situation itself?

According to our research, approximately seven in ten people who are not financially struggling still say they suffer financial stress, with nearly one in ten reporting high or overwhelming financial stress.

They may not be carrying high levels of debt or living paycheck to paycheck, but their finances still stress them out, and the impact of that still wreaks havoc on their physical and mental health. Stress doesn't discriminate—the cortisol it releases day in and day out is equally toxic regardless of the seriousness of the situation.

Obviously, for people who are financially stable but still experiencing financial stress—for example, they are feeling like they aren't progressing enough or are worrying about losing the money they do have due to an economic downturn—the stress reduction techniques described in Chapter 5 are critical. Simply getting perspective on the fact your situation isn't a true financial crisis can automatically reduce your stress. But just as is the case for people who are struggling, those who are financially stable but still dealing with high levels of financial stress can also benefit from addressing the underlying financial situation causing the stress.

Those who are financially stable fall into one of the final two categories—planning and optimizing—with each having a different set of financial stressors.

PLANNING

First, let's address those in the planning category. People in this category have a strong financial foundation and are in the process of working toward key financial goals like buying a home, saving for their children's education expenses, building a nest egg to become more financially independent, or achieving any number of other goals that are important to building the life they want for themselves and their loved ones. Their main causes of stress are feeling like they aren't making progress fast enough, due to either life in general or financial setbacks that make it harder for them to fund goals—everything from emergencies that temporarily limit their ability to save to market downturns that cause them to lose money in their key savings accounts, compromising their ability to reach their goal in the time frame they originally intended.

How to Address Stress from Challenges to Reaching Your Financial Goals

Ultimately, there are four major things you can do to close the gap between where you are and where you want to be with respect to achieving key financial goals:

1. **Save more by cutting other expenses.** If the goal is very important and it is relatively easy to find expenses to cut without compromising your quality of life, then this is probably the best route. Depending on the goal, as little as a few dollars a day can often make the difference between achieving it in the time frame you want and having to delay by a few years.

2. **Change the scale of the goal.** If you don't have much room to cut expenses or the goal is important but not to the level that requires sacrificing your current lifestyle, then the next best thing to do is to reevaluate the scale of the goal. For example, if you want to buy a home, you set the goal based on your vision of an ideal home for yourself and your loved ones and arrive at what you would need to save to achieve this vision. It's worth rethinking that vision to see if there are compromises you can make that still get you a home that is a safe, happy place for you and your family to live. If the neighborhood is important to you, maybe the compromise is square footage. If the square footage is important to you, maybe it's about finding a different neighborhood—or different location altogether—where you can get more space without compromising other things that are important, like being safe, being in a good school district, or having a backyard for your children and/or pets. *Bottom line:* If you can still get most of what you want by changing the scale of the goal, it's usually better to do this than delay the goal altogether.

3. **Delay your goal.** When my team and I discuss this option with most people, they typically resist it initially—and that's understandable. No one wants to delay reaching a major financial

goal that they've been looking forward to for years. However, if you are going to have to make significant changes in your lifestyle in order to reach your goal and a scaled-down goal is not an option because it requires sacrificing what you truly want for yourself or your family, then this is probably the best option, provided the goal is not time sensitive (like sending children to college).

4. **Change your investment strategy for your goal.** This is listed fourth for a reason: It is risky and could backfire, as the market is not predictable. However, if you have a long-term goal (10 or more years away) and you are investing very conservatively—putting most or all of that money in a savings account, CD, or money market account, you are putting yourself in a situation where your money is set up to grow very slowly, and this may hold you back from being able to achieve your goal within the time frame you've set. To rectify this, you may want to consider taking more risk by investing a portion of your savings in mutual funds that hold stocks, bonds, or a combination of both. This will set you up for the likelihood (the key word here is "likelihood"—there are no guarantees) of being able to grow your money faster so that you can meet your goal on time. To determine the best way to invest your money, based on both your risk tolerance and the time horizon for your goal, go to www.ffcalcs.com/risk_assessment.

OPTIMIZING

People in the optimizing category are those who have already reached a high level of financial security and are at or very close to full financial independence—meaning they have amassed a sufficient enough nest egg to sustain their current lifestyle for decades. You would think that these people would never face financial stress—the same way you assume people who visibly are physically fit don't worry about their health.

The reality is that while people in the optimizing category are less likely than people in all other financial categories to face high or overwhelming financial stress, many of them still struggle with financial stress for a very interesting phenomenon called "loss aversion." Studies show we are much more sensitive to the risks of losing money than the rewards of building wealth.

Nobel Prize–winning economist Daniel Kahneman and his associate Amos Tversky originally identified loss aversion in 1979. Studies on loss aversion have shown that the pain of a loss is often twice as intense as the pleasure of an equivalent gain.

Kahneman illustrated how this plays out in a simple experiment he did with his students: He told them that if a flipped coin lands on tails, they would lose $10. Then he asked them how much they would need to win to make the coin flip worth the risk of losing $10. The answer, he said, was typically more than $20. Rationally, this makes no sense. Anything over $10 would put the odds in your favor mathematically, but most people required double that to even be willing to take the chance because of their fear of losing.

Because of loss aversion, optimizers can be prone to worry about losing the wealth they have built, particularly if they grew up in poverty, sustained significant financial losses in the past, or have a high level of anxiety in general.

Again, the stress reduction techniques in Chapter 5 can be really valuable to people in this category to provide a sense of perspective and even gratitude and remind them that they are, in fact, in a strong financial position.

But that's not the only remedy. Sometimes people that work so hard to reach financial independence lose it because they don't take the proper steps to protect the wealth they've built. This may force retirees back to work. A Federal Reserve Board Study shows that fully one-third of those that retire end up reentering the workforce.[3]

So the best thing those in this category can do is something that everyone should be doing—bulletproof their finances. Optimizers have more to do in this area than others because they have more assets and more complex financial situations. But all people who are not in a financial crisis should take steps to bulletproof their finances so they are protected from whatever happens to the economy or market or whatever personal setbacks they face. We will discuss how you can bulletproof your finances in Chapter 8.

7

NAVIGATING FINANCIALLY STRESSFUL LIFE EVENTS

I f you are not currently facing a life event that is creating significant financial stress, you can skip this chapter and move on to Chapter 8 to learn how to bulletproof your finances.

If you are dealing with a significant life event that has upended your finances, please read on. Given how emotionally and financially draining unexpected life events can be, as well as the level of complexity in terms of the decisions you have to make to get through them as smoothly as possible, they merit a chapter of their own.

One thing that I want to be really clear about here. This is not about the "life happens" emergencies we all face, which can be stressful at the time, but are generally relatively easy to bounce back from, things like the car breaking down, the roof leaking, the dog unexpectedly getting sick.

What I'm referring to here are life-changing financial emergencies that are far more expensive and disruptive to your finances and require that you make a series of informed financial decisions to get to a point of resolution and reduce your financial stress as a result. These may not be as traumatic as Melissa's story of losing everything and having to rebuild from scratch, but they have the potential to temporarily wreak havoc on your finances, especially if you don't take the right steps to navigate the emergencies to minimize the financial pain.

Life-changing financial emergencies might be enormous medical expenses related to serious diseases or illnesses where the best treatment simply costs more than insurance will cover and you have to go into debt to pay for it, or major life events like divorce, the death of a spouse, or a disability that completely upends your finances.

Here are some of the most common life events that create financial distress and what you can do to overcome them and reach financial stability.

LOSS OF A JOB

- **Figure out what you're entitled to.** If you were laid off as part of a larger labor reduction or early retirement program, chances are you will be offered some type of severance based on your years of service and job level. There are a lot of factors to keep in mind, so make sure you understand how it all works before you accept your package. Make sure to read and fully understand your entire severance agreement before you sign it. Work with your HR team to get all your outstanding pay, including any vacation or sick pay. Apply for unemployment benefits if you are eligible.

- **Be sure you are covered by health insurance.** If losing your job also means losing your health insurance, this should be your top priority. The last thing you want is a medical emergency that compounds the financial challenges you are already facing due to losing your job. Find out what COBRA coverage would cost to keep your current insurance in place for up to 18 months. Explore going on your spouse's plan, as a change in your job status is considered a qualifying event. Research the cost of coverage through an individual broker and compare your options with medical sharing plans and the federal Health Insurance Marketplace®.

- **Decide what to do with any retirement savings.** If you have money in a retirement plan (e.g., 401(k)) and/or a pension benefit, you will likely have several different options: Leave it there, roll it into an IRA (individual retirement account), transfer it to your next employer, or withdraw the funds subject to taxes and penalties. In some cases, the best option is to either keep your retirement savings where it is or roll it over to your new employer's retirement plan. Pay attention to fees! Depending on how high your balance is and how much time you have until you plan to withdraw the funds, higher fees could be a difference of tens of thousands, or even hundreds of thousands, of dollars over time. Keeping your money in a retirement plan will likely protect it from creditors, bankruptcy proceedings, and civil lawsuits. Furthermore, employers have a legal responsibility to offer investments that are appropriate for their employees. This doesn't mean there are no risks—not all employers take this responsibility as seriously as they should— but it adds a layer of protection not available if you choose to manage your own investments in an IRA.

- **Evaluate your budget, and cut back where you need to.** Chances are that money will be tight in the short term due to your loss of income, so be conservative with your spending while you're out of work to stretch your savings as long as you can. Be brutally honest about "needs" versus "wants," and stick to a strict spending plan. Cancel or pause any unnecessary services, and place any monthly memberships on hold. Use your emergency fund to fill any gaps, and try to avoid taking on new debt. Consider short-term alternatives to make some extra cash, like doing temp or consulting work, driving for a rideshare company, or renting out an extra room. Explore selling your home or moving to a cheaper place if you're in a tough job market.

- **Contact creditors if you're having difficulty paying.** As long as you give advance notice, most banks and credit card companies are willing to work with you during tough times to keep your account in good standing even if you can't make your full payments. The key is that you must let them know *before* you can't pay. If you've missed a payment, they may not be as understanding, and your credit score will take a hit right when you need it to be the best it can be. Make a list of all your creditors—mortgage holder, credit card companies, student loan provider, car loan company, etc. Contact each one to learn more about your options due to job loss. Prioritize paying your housing, car note, and insurance bills first if you have to make choices about which to pay.

- **Set yourself up for success in a new role.** You may feel under pressure to take the first job that comes by, but don't rush it. If the position you are considering is not at a company that you respect, or if the company does not offer fair compensation and benefits or solid career prospects, you may find yourself back in the job market faster than you'd like. Know your worth by researching compensation and benefits for companies in your area, and don't be afraid to negotiate any offers.

MEDICAL EMERGENCIES

- **Before you get a medical procedure, find out the average cost.** Even though your doctor may be covered by your insurance, the facility where you are getting your procedure may not be, so be sure to verify insurance coverage. The price of a procedure can cost three times or more as much at one facility versus another. Call local hospitals or use websites like Healthcare Bluebook to gauge how much your medical bill may cost.[1] Finally, try to negotiate the cost of your procedure before you get the service. Even after you have your procedure, still do a cost comparison. If your bill is much higher than the average for your area, use that information to negotiate your medical bill.

- **Contact your provider ASAP if you cannot afford to pay.** Many hospitals have programs for people who are uninsured or underinsured. The billing office may be able to find alternative ways to pay for the bill. In addition, ask the hospital for a written financial assistance policy. The policy should spell out eligibility and the process of applying for assistance. Make sure any deals and/or discounts you get are in writing as well.

- **Evaluate all sources of funds to cover your bills.** When it comes to paying for medical bills, the first place to look for funds is your HSA (health savings account) or healthcare FSA (flexible spending account). If you still need additional funds, consider using your emergency savings (if you have established an emergency savings fund), drawing from other investment accounts, or taking a loan or hardship withdrawal from a retirement account. Last, you can check if your employer has a benevolence fund for employees experiencing a hardship.

- **After your procedure, ask for an itemized bill and your medical records.** Medical bills are notorious for errors. Any items on your bill that do not match your medical records should be disputed.

- **Consider hiring a medical bill negotiator.** If you've done all the negotiating you can on your own but still need help with your bill, a professional may be able to save you a lot of time and money. Some companies charge by the hour. Others charge as a percentage of savings. You can search for a medical bill negotiator on websites like the National Association of Healthcare Advocacy,[2] the Alliance of Claims Assistance Professionals,[3] and the Patient Advocate Foundation.[4]

- **Shop around for prescription medication.** The same drug can vary wildly in price depending on where you go to get the medication.[5] This is because the price of the drug typically depends on the pharmacy's deal with the supplier, the pharmacist's overhead, and profit margins. Check prices at different pharmacies or use websites like GoodRx.com or RxSaver.com to shop around for the best price in your area. Typically, you do not need to be a member of warehouses like Costco or Sam's Club to use their pharmacies.

DIVORCE

- **Begin establishing your independent financial identity.** You've likely been linked with your spouse via many of your financial accounts to this point, so you need to start separating yourself financially as soon as possible. Try to work with your former spouse to close all joint bank accounts, and open your own checking accounts, making sure to update any direct deposits. If possible, close all joint credit cards and loans, and transfer the balances to accounts in your individual names. Be prepared for your credit score to drop as you close lines of credit, but understand it's the only way to separate your credit from your spouse's, and you can always reopen additional lines of credit to improve your score after taking this step. Review your credit report for all joint debt, and notify creditors of your separation. Notify insurance providers to establish policies in your name.

- **Work to get a fair settlement.** You may want to just "get it over with," but you should take your time to ensure that the final settlement is fair to both sides, so you don't regret it later. Try to keep your future self in mind throughout the process, and stand up for yourself, but also know when to let go if things get petty. Hire an attorney to represent your interests. Make a list of all your property under three columns: "I keep," "Spouse keeps," and "To be determined." Write down your other priorities regarding finances and your children.

- **Review your tax situation.** Once your divorce is final, you'll need to file as a single or head of household taxpayer for that entire year, which could cause an unusually high tax refund or balance due if you don't make adjustments accordingly. Update your W-4 with HR to reflect your new marital status and any changes in dependents. If your parenting agreement includes a provision where you will be claiming a dependent every other year, you may need to update your W-4 annually.

■ **Update your estate plan and insurance policies.** A divorce is a "qualifying event," which means you can adjust your benefits for a limited time after that occurs. As soon as practically possible, you'll want to remove your ex-spouse from all policies and documents or obtain the proper coverage on your own. It can be a tedious process, so take it one step at a time, but don't put it off. Update beneficiary forms for retirement accounts, life insurance, HSAs, stock purchase plans, etc. Draft a new will. Make appropriate changes to your health, life, and/ or disability insurance. Check to see if your EAP (employee assistance program) provides legal assistance for drafting a new will and other estate planning documents. Your estate planning documents can have an enormous impact on your beneficiaries' futures. For example, if you have minor children with your ex and you pass away with your children listed as beneficiaries, there is a high likelihood that your ex, their parent and guardian, will have control over the funds until they reach adulthood. If you have any concerns about the implications of this, you should talk to an estate planning attorney to explore a trust that your ex will not have control over.

■ **Plan how you'll manage the final settlement terms.** The purpose of a divorce settlement is to ensure that each of you receives your fair share of any savings toward long-term goals. If you are receiving a settlement, use the money to establish a firm financial foundation as you rebuild your financial life. If you are paying the settlement, take the time to revisit your spending habits and savings goals, as it'll be time well spent. If necessary, establish an IRA to receive retirement plan distributions paid out because of a QDRO (qualified domestic relations order). Determine if your house will be sold or how the mortgage balance will be addressed if one of you will be staying in the home. Pay down any high interest rate debt with nonretirement settlement funds. Invest any funds you won't need for 10 years or more for long-term growth.

- **Create a postdivorce plan.** Going from two incomes to one and possibly establishing yourself in a new home will likely require a complete overhaul of your budget. Make sure you are able to take care of your short-term needs, but also start to think about how your long-term goals may have shifted. Create your postdivorce budget. Plan out alimony and/or child support cash payments, keeping in mind major milestones. Make a plan to pay off any debt you're bringing from your marriage. Run a retirement calculator (see Figure 7.1) to make sure you get back on track. You'll find a retirement calculator you can use at https://www.ffcalcs.com/retirement_estimator.

DEATH OF A SPOUSE

- **Get help processing and coping with your loss.** Grief can make it difficult to manage your finances, so it is important to get support with your loss if you are feeling overwhelmed or depressed. If you are employed, look into your company's EAP. Most EAPs offer free counseling sessions where you can talk to a therapist, as well as a referral program if you want a longer-term solution after you've used up the free sessions. Many even have specific grief counseling for people who have lost a spouse, so inquire about whether that service is available as part of your EAP benefit.

- **Assess your day-to-day spending needs.** While you should postpone major financial decisions, you'll need to take stock pretty quickly of your income and expenses in order to keep

Retirement Estimator

This calculator will help you to estimate how much your retirement accounts could be worth at retirement. It will also tell you if you appear to be on track to achieve your retirement income goal based on information you provide.

| Profile | Retirement Plan | Retirement income | Other Assets | Goal Calculation | Next Steps |

Introduction

Use this calculator to see if you are on track to retire at your desired retirement age based on your current retirement savings plan and investment approach. Have questions about this calculator? Find out How To Run A Retirement Estimate.

Settings

Tax Year

2022

Spouse Option ●

Calculate for Myself Only ⌄

Income Replacement Target ●

80%

You		**Your Spouse / Partner**	
Current Age	Retirement Age	Current Age	Retirement Age
35	65	35	65
Life Expectancy ●		Life Expectancy ●	
85		85	
Annual Salary + Bonus		Annual Salary + Bonus	
$0		$0	

next »

FIGURE 7.1   Sample retirement calculator

your finances going, especially if your spouse was the primary financial person in your family. Make a list of all income sources and fixed expenses. Note which income sources will decline or go away, like your spouse's income. Determine whether you need to cut back on discretionary spending until things are settled. Cancel any of your spouse's accounts you decide you no longer need, like mobile phone, club memberships, or other subscriptions. Obtain access to your spouse's email to be sure you don't miss any bill notifications or other financial statements.

■ **Hire an attorney if you don't already have one.** Work with your attorney to begin the estate settlement process. Getting accounts and other property transferred out of your spouse's name may take some time, especially if your spouse ran the household finances. By gathering as much of the information ahead of time like statements and other account information, you can minimize the frustration of updating accounts and property ownership as well as lessen the legal costs for your attorney's assistance. Obtain multiple copies of the death certificate—one for each account, plus several extra.

■ **Collect life insurance proceeds.** You don't have to wait for any probate process to be settled before you can collect any life insurance payable to you. If you don't have an agent or aren't sure where the policies are held, go through bank account statements to see if there are any transactions to an insurance company in the past year. Contact your spouse's employer about any company-provided life insurance and file a claim. Check with any professional or fraternal organizations where your spouse was a member to see if any group policies were purchased. Consult an unbiased financial planner if you are unsure what to do with the proceeds.

■ **Decide when you want to claim Social Security survivor benefits.** A widow or widower may be entitled to a survivor benefit of up to 100 percent of the deceased spouse's benefit. If you have minor children, they may also qualify for survivor benefits until they reach age 18. Find out what your benefit would be if you claimed today as survivor versus if you waited until full retirement age to make the claim. Make your filing decision based on benefit amounts and your income needs.

■ **Make any necessary changes to auto, homeowners, or any other insurance policies that covered your spouse.** If you were covered under your spouse's health insurance, you'll need to elect COBRA and/or find new coverage. Enroll in your employer's health insurance if available, as losing a spouse is a qualifying event that allows for mid-year enrollment. Compare COBRA with Health Insurance Marketplace® plans if you don't have coverage available through work. Consider increasing your own life insurance if you still have dependent children, and update beneficiaries, if necessary.

- **Update your estate planning documents.** This is an important time to reassess how your assets would be distributed and identify who can make decisions for you if you are not able to make them yourself.

- **Assess your long-term care needs.** It's possible that you and your spouse had intended to care for each other, so you will need to find another option if that was the case. Look at your family history to assess the likelihood of needing long-term care, and plan accordingly either by purchasing long-term care insurance or setting aside funds to cover the estimated costs, which run around $80,000 per year for an average of three years for those who want to stay in a facility that provides excellent care.

DISABILITY

- **Get an idea of how long you will be out of work.** Ask your doctor for worst-case and best-case timelines; then shoot for best case with your recovery, but plan for worst case with your personal finances. The last thing you need is to feel the financial pressure of going back to work before you're fully ready and able. Find out how disability leave works at your company. Notify HR, and provide any paperwork necessary from your doctor. Contact your EAP, if available, to explore resources offered.

- **Explore your eligibility for disability payments.** You may be eligible for coverage under your employer's disability policy, your own policy if you have one, and/or Social Security, so make sure you explore all your options to help pay your bills while you're out of work. Check into workers' compensation if you were injured at work. Find out how much your short-term and long-term disability policies pay and how they define a disability. Learn when the waiting periods and coverage periods end. Apply for Social Security benefits if your disability is severe and permanent.

- **Evaluate your budget, and cut back where you need to.** If money is tight, you may have to take an axe to your spending while you're out of work. Figure out what expenses you can temporarily trim until your income is back to normal. Be brutally honest about needs versus wants. Cancel any unnecessary services, and place any monthly memberships on hold. Use your emergency fund to fill any gaps to try to avoid taking on new debt. Look into federally funded programs such as LIHEAP (Low Income Home Energy Assistance Program) to help pay for heating and cooling bills if necessary.

- **Contact creditors if you're having difficulty paying.** (If the advice here sounds familiar, that's because the same advice was given above for when you lose a job.) As long as you give advance notice, most banks and credit card companies are willing to work with you during tough times to keep your account in good standing even if you can't make your full payments. The key is that you must let them know *before* you can't pay. If you've missed a payment, they may not be as understanding, and your credit score will take a hit. Make a list of all your creditors—mortgage holder, credit card companies, student loan provider, car loan company, etc. Contact each one to learn more about their disability or income loss programs. Prioritize paying your housing, car note, and insurance bills first if you have to make choices about what to pay.

EXERCISE

If your financial struggles are a result of a financially devastating life event, outline the steps you plan to take to recover based on what you've learned from this section. If possible, enlist the support of a financial coach or someone you trust to go through this process with you so you don't have to bear the weight of this responsibility by yourself.

8

BULLETPROOFING YOUR FINANCES

Once you get to a place where you are past your financial challenges and stressors, there's one final step that is absolutely critical, and that is to do what we call "bulletproofing your finances."

Bulletproofing your finances means doing exactly what it implies—fully protecting yourself from financial harm—putting yourself in a position to withstand whatever unexpected challenges might come your way in the future. In our experience, most people miss this step in the process of tackling their financial stress. They are so relieved to simply get through their financial challenges and reduce their financial stress that they feel like their problems are resolved and it will be smooth sailing in the future. The problem is that we have no idea of what life is going to throw our way. The only thing that is pretty much certain is that you will face unexpected financial challenges in the form of big and small emergencies, downturns in the economy or stock market, unexpected tax bills, or even lawsuits. And when those things happen, the way to ensure they don't derail your finances is to bulletproof your finances.

Below is a guide that will provide you with steps to take to bullet-proof your finances based on your current financial situation, using three of the categories we established earlier in Chapter 6: struggling, planning, and optimizing. As you progress financially from one category to another, you'll want to come back and review these steps to make sure you have the right level of protection in place to ensure your finances are as "bulletproof" as possible.

STRUGGLING

- **Build an emergency fund.** The emergency fund is your safety net to avoid getting into a difficult financial situation due to loss of income and significant, unexpected, one-time expenses. Having an emergency fund in place can reduce stress, anxiety, and other emotions that often make handling the nonfinancial aspects of an emergency much more difficult. The general rule of thumb is save three to six months' worth of your living expenses. However, you can always start with a goal you find achievable. Say, for example, $1,000. Once you reach that goal, aim for three months of rent, then three months of the next highest essential expense, and so on. *Remember, you can always start small.* If you have not started your fund, consider putting $25 from every paycheck into a savings account designated for emergencies. Then check your budget or spending plan to see how much you can save after you've paid essential expenses and before budgeting for discretionary spending.

- **Don't add to your debt.** If possible, use your credit cards sparingly (but don't close the accounts—that could impact your credit) and use a debit card instead for all purchases you make at stores. To ensure you don't end up making online transactions using your credit cards, consider removing your credit card details from your electronic wallet in your phone and within sites that you use regularly to shop, and input your debit card details as a replacement. Avoid taking out even low interest rate debt unless it's absolutely necessary (e.g., if you need to buy a car for work purposes and have to get a loan to do so) until you become more financially stable and are in a position where you are actively saving for future financial goals.

- **Make sure you effectively manage your healthcare so you are well covered in the event you need significant medical attention.** If you are in a high-deductible plan, make sure you have money set aside in your HSA to cover your deductible. Make sure that the plan covers medical care you need or expect to need so you don't have to pay out of pocket. During open enrollment at work, be sure to do a thorough comparison of your healthcare options to be sure you have the best coverage for your needs at the lowest cost. This does not mean automatically choosing the insurance with the lowest premium. That may be the best option if you are young, single, and extremely healthy; but the more complex your life is in terms of needing family coverage or needing coverage for chronic conditions or specific prescriptions, you are typically better off with plans that are more comprehensive and have good coverage of your healthcare needs. Often your employer will provide tools/resources to help you compare.

- **Make sure you are covered in the event of a disability.** One in three employees will face disability at one point in their lives, and the financial impacts can be devastating if you don't have disability insurance.

- **Make sure your insurance coverage is in order.** In most states, you need car insurance, but even if it's not mandatory, you should have it if you drive, because a major accident can completely derail your finances if you are found to be at fault. If you own a home, you probably were required to get homeowners insurance when you secured your mortgage. Review your policy, and make sure it covers the full value of your home and covers fires, flooding, and other natural disasters that could literally destroy your home. If you rent and the value of your furnishings, appliances, and other possessions in your home would be very costly to replace, make sure you have a renters insurance policy in place. If you have a spouse and/or children whom you support financially, make sure that you have sufficient life insurance in place so they will be able to continue to fund their living expenses in the event you pass away. The best place to start is by reviewing what your employer offers for free and then looking at options to supplement your free coverage through group rates that are typically more favorable than what you will find outside your employer in the retail marketplace.

■ **Have a basic will in place to ensure that the things you care most about are designated to go to the people you want to receive them.** If you have children, make sure you have a plan for guardianship. This is particularly important if you are raising your children alone. But even if you have a spouse or partner, it's good to intentionally designate them as the guardian, and have a backup in place in the event that person passes or becomes disabled and cannot care for your children.

PLANNING

Obviously, when you are in the planning stage, you will need to do everything that someone who is struggling is doing, to make sure you have your fundamentals covered. But you'll also have to ensure that you are taking the best possible steps to protect your financial goals, so that your goals are properly protected and you are limiting the risks of not being able to achieve them at the scale or in the time frame that is important to you and your family.

For people in this category, bulletproofing typically comes down to these two steps: (1) making sure you have an effective *plan* and (2) making sure you have an effective *planning process* in place.

Let's start with the first step: having an effective plan. With each goal, you will want to make sure you are taking a relatively conservative approach when you plan so that if you encounter higher-than-expected inflation or low or declining investment returns, you will still be in a strong position to reach your goal with minimal disruption to your finances. This means trying to save about 10 to 20 percent more than a financial calculator indicates you need to save, and automating that process so that you are automatically diverting money from each paycheck into a separate account for that goal. For short-term goals (less than 5 years), you shouldn't be taking on any investment risk—stick to money market accounts, CDs, or savings accounts so you can be assured that your money is safe and protected from the ups and downs of the economy or stock market. For longer-term goals, you can take more risk, especially if the goal is more than 10 years away, but you will want to make sure you are investing in line with your risk tolerance, so you don't panic and sell your investments when the market drops, locking in losses. Use the Investor Risk Profile & Allocation Worksheet (www.ffcalcs.com/risk_assessment) to assess your risk tolerance and make decisions about which investments are best for you based on that.

The next step in bulletproofing your goals is all about making sure you have an effective planning process in place. You should review how you are doing relative to each goal at least once a year (more frequently if you go through major financial changes) and make adjustments as needed. If possible, you should save more if you are encountering high levels of inflation or if the market has dropped and you are behind where you want to be; the idea is to change your investment strategy as needed. We'll talk more about how to do this in the next module. The important takeaway here is to stay on top of your goals so that you don't get into a situation where you discover too late that you are too far behind to catch up in time to fully fund your goals.

OPTIMIZING

The biggest threat to optimizers, who are mostly or fully financially independent, is what we discussed earlier—losing the wealth they've built. If you are in this category, you experience the most stress when the economy goes into a recession, the market crashes, or inflation soars—all of which can cause your net worth to take a significant hit. While this is a considerably better problem to have than the kind of challenges that those who are financially struggling—or even those in the planning phase—have to deal with, it can be very unnerving to see your wealth decline by 10, 20, 30, or 40 percent or more (even if the losses are paper losses—meaning you haven't sold your investments and they will likely rebound over time).

The best way to manage these risks—which you can't control but can definitely mitigate—are to take the following steps:

- **Ensure you are properly diversified so that your wealth isn't tied up in a single investment or market sector.** We'll discuss this more in later chapters, but the biggest reason that people who have reached financial security lose it is because they take on way too much investment risk. Then, when the value of their narrowly concentrated investments plummets, they end up in a situation where they are forced to sell at a low; or worse, they're in a situation where whatever they were invested in loses most or all of its value (most common if your money is tied up in a single company's stock). Think of Enron, WorldCom, Pets.com, or any number of other high-flying investments that literally lost all their value.

- **Ensure that you are protecting yourself from fraud. Avoid the temptation to invest in sophisticated investments you don't understand that promise strong returns.** More often than not, it's a sign of fraud when any financial professional selling an investment guarantees a return that is well above what savings or money market accounts provide, and you should avoid these investments like the plague. Use caution when giving someone full discretion—meaning the ability to buy and sell investments without your permission—over your accounts. Establish guidelines to protect you from a financial planner taking undue risk with your money. And back to the first point above, diversify wisely. If, God forbid, you do end up becoming a victim of a fraudulent investment, it's much easier to recover if you are well diversified and the investment is a small percentage of your overall wealth.

- **Make sure that you are protected from lawsuits or other financial catastrophes.** Insurance takes on much more significance when you have more assets to protect. Work with a financial planner you trust to make sure you are properly insured. If your income is driving much of your wealth and you have dependents, life insurance becomes even more important to make sure their standard of living will continue after you are gone. You will also want to have very strong disability insurance coverage, because becoming disabled will compromise your ability to work and to make the income needed to support your lifestyle, and you want to avoid draining your savings and investment accounts. Last, umbrella liability insurance is a must for most people who have amassed a significant nest egg. The reality is that we live in a lawsuit-happy society, where something as seemingly innocent as someone getting injured falling down the stairs in your house at a party can be cause for a lawsuit. Even the most frivolous lawsuits can accrue significant legal expenses—these are the ones where you don't go to trial but where you can end up having to pay large settlement expenses.

- **Hire an excellent accountant who can intentionally work with you to minimize your tax liability. In rare circumstances, you can end up owing more taxes than you have cash on hand to pay the taxes.** This happens most often with stock options or grants, where you may end up with a large tax liability based on gains in the stock price even if you haven't sold the stock. The right accountant will make sure that you don't end up in this position and that you take intentional steps to protect your wealth from taxes in general.

- **Last but not least, you'll want to hire a financial planner to help you put all the above plans in place, and ensure your wealth is protected from additional risks specific to your**

personal financial situation. The reason this point is listed last is that it's important that you are aware of the above steps first. To get the best results with any financial planner, you should be an active participant in the process—which means knowing what you want to accomplish and having enough financial knowledge to be able to effectively manage the relationship with the financial planner you choose to hire. To find a financial planner that has the breadth of knowledge and experience to ensure that you have a comprehensive wealth preservation plan in place (essentially what bulletproofing means when you are an optimizer), go to www.letsmakeaplan.org. There you can find CERTIFIED FINANCIAL PLANNER™ professionals in your local area who have experience in the areas where you need the most guidance.

9

FOR THOSE FACING A SERIOUS FINANCIAL CRISIS

I f this is your situation and you are employed, the best thing you can do is use resources your employer has available. Ask your HR representative at your company for help, and specifically find out if the company has any of the following available:

1. A foundation or fund to help employees in severe financial crisis—where you can get a quick grant to get you through the hardship you are facing and back on your feet.

2. A financial coaching benefit where you can get connected with a financial coach who can work with you to determine the best possible way to handle the situation—whether that's working with your landlord or other creditors to negotiate more time to come up with money for rent or to pay other needed bills, tapping into community resources you may not be aware of that are designed to help people in your situation, or leveraging other company benefits designed to help employees in need; basically it's finding a way to get more time to pay your bills and getting

temporary support to sustain yourself and your loved ones. A good financial coach will know what is available to you based on where you live, and will help advocate for you so you don't get lost in the red tape.

3. An EAP (employee assistance program). Almost every company has an EAP that you can call to get immediate help around any sort of crisis situation. When you connect with your EAP, ask what it has available in terms of connections to immediate resources that can help your situation—from credit counseling to connections to programs that can provide immediate financial assistance or relief.

If you are not employed and are facing a financial crisis, you'll want to turn to charitable and government resources that you can secure quickly. A lot of people feel a sense of deep shame about going this route, but the reality is that these programs exist for a reason—to help well-intentioned people who are in financial hardship get back on their feet. And you are in good company, as unemployment aid is very common. In the COVID-19 pandemic alone, one in four workers relied on unemployment benefits. Over the course of a full working life, many will need to use this safety net at one point or another.

HOW TO ACCESS GOVERNMENT BENEFITS

To better understand the government benefits available to you, check out the Government Benefits website at https://www.usa.gov/benefits. This site lists all the government programs that can help with food, housing, healthcare, and other basic living expenses. If you need additional help beyond resources available through your employer or government aid, the next section includes a list of excellent resources that can help you keep your home, provide for your family, and get back on your feet financially until you are able to become more financially secure using the START™ framework.

OTHER BENEFITS AND RESOURCES FOR IMMEDIATE NEEDS (HOUSING, FOOD, CHILDCARE)

In addition to government benefits, you'll want to check out the programs listed below to see if they can help you with temporary funding, housing, or other resources to get you through your financial crisis:

- **Need Help Paying Bills** (https://www.needhelppayingbills.com). This site has put together a great collection of resources for all types of assistance programs, categorized and explained by the type of assistance needed and available to you.
- **United Way 2-1-1** (https://www.211.org). Find your local affiliate at this site to see whom it partners with in your community.
- **Community Action Partnership** (https://www.community actionpartnership.com/find-a-cap). Search for your local Community Action Agency for local help.
- **Salvation Army** (https://www.salvationarmyusa.org/usn). Search for local resources by city or zip code.
- **Feeding America** (https://www.feedingamerica.org/find-your -local-foodbank). Find your local food bank through this site.
- **The Society of St. Vincent de Paul** (https://www.svdpusa.org/ Assistance-Services/). Find your local society, and explore the resources available in your area.
- **NFCC** (https://www.nfcc.org). For credit counseling help that won't scam you, contact the National Foundation for Credit Counseling.
- **LIHEAP** (https://www.acf.hhs.gov/ocs/map/liheap-map-state -and-territory-contact-listing). For state-based assistance with heating or cooling your home, find your state's program on this site.
- **WIC** (https://www.fns.usda.gov/wic). To apply for nutritional assistance for you and your children, contact WIC through the federal government.

ADDITIONAL OPTIONS

- **Utilities.** Most utility providers have programs funded by the United Way or donations from neighbors in your own community. Apply on the utility company's website or contact the company directly for temporary assistance with gas, electric, and water utilities.
- **Hospitals.** Some offer assistance programs funded by donors, so ask the billing department if that's an option. Don't delay though; some have deadlines such as 90 to 180 days to apply.
- **Prescriptions.** If your situation is short term, ask your medical providers if they can provide free prescription samples temporarily. Most want to ensure you don't neglect your health and will have some available. If longer term, reach out to the pharmaceutical companies that make the medications; many have patient assistance programs that offer free or discounted medicines.
- **Family and friends.** Asking for help can feel uncomfortable at first, but you may find that those closest to you are willing— even wanting—to help.

EXERCISE

If you are employed and have a financial coaching program or employee assistance program available as an employee benefit, call them immediately. In some cases, they can help you find relief within a matter of days, sometimes quicker. They may also be able to direct you to resources that work on your behalf to negotiate with your landlord or mortgage company to secure more time to pay overdue bills, working with other creditors to secure more favorable payment terms, or working with different community resources to ensure that you are able to get support as quickly as possible.

If you are not employed, look at the lists of resources above and determine which are the best fit for you based on your immediate needs. If possible, enlist someone you trust to help you go through this process, so you can get through it faster and also have the emotional support to make the process less stressful.

Module 3

ADVANCE TOWARD THE LIFE YOU WANT

ABOUT THIS MODULE

After you set yourself up for financial success and put a plan in place to reduce your financial stress and overcome your financial challenges, it's time to turn your attention to the fun part—which is taking the steps to build the life you want. In this module, you'll learn how to do this in a way that doesn't compromise your self-care, which is critical to making sure you can sustain the progress you make.

We'll also take you through an exercise to envision the life you want—something that is easier said than done—because you'll really have to examine what your most important priorities are today, which may be different than what you grew up thinking was important or what society tells you is important. From there, you'll learn how you can create a master plan for your goals that (1) is realistic based on your budget and (2) ensures the preservation of your self-care needs, which never should be compromised for longer-term goals.

This module ends with specific guidance on how to achieve the individual goals you've determined are critically important to attaining the life you want, so you have a step-by-step guide to achieve each goal.

10

FINANCIAL SELF-CARE

Most financial planners will focus you on the long term, but life is a combination of enjoying the present as much as you can and planning for the future. And if you go too far on the planning end, you can end up depriving yourself of the things that make you happiest today, and most importantly, the things that sustain your physical and mental well-being. Obviously, if you are in a state of crisis, where your mental well-being is already compromised by virtue of the level of stress you are facing, you need to focus all your efforts on getting back on your feet. But when that is not the case, you should always make sure you are spending the time and money needed to properly take care of yourself. Without properly taking care of yourself, you will eventually end up in a mental (and possibly physical) state that causes major setbacks—both financially and otherwise. So before you even plan for the future, think about how to create a strong foundation that ensures you are able to maintain a healthy financial mindset that you need to progress financially. You cannot build upon a weak foundation; everything crumbles.

Self-care is different for all of us. For most it's a combination of habits and some degree of financial investment to ensure that we manage our stress, intentionally take care of our physical and mental health, and maintain a positive mindset toward our future.

At the end of the day, self-care is all about boundaries and nonne-gotiables. When you are financially struggling, you may have less money to devote to things that keep you mentally and physically healthy and instead find ways to leverage resources provided by your employer for things like therapy (again looking into the employee assistance program for counseling). Or you might learn meditation or yoga through an app or YouTube video, practice techniques to get enough sleep, and make sure you refuel by spending quality time with your friends and family. These all can be done for relatively little cost but can make a big dif-ference to your peace of mind and sense of perspective, all of which are critical to sustaining and building upon the financial progress you make.

When you do progress financially, you can carve out a self-care budget that includes therapy; vacations to unwind and get away from the pres-sures of work and daily life; and/or preventive health practices like acu-puncture, workouts at the gym, or even a session or two with a nutritionist to create a healthier diet. I can't tell you what works for you to maintain your perspective and sense of well-being, but I do recommend that as you progress financially, you allocate a portion of your budget to investing in the things that provide you the most benefit mentally, physically, and emo-tionally. If you don't take care of yourself, you will eventually burn out, and that almost always results in sabotaging the progress you've made because you end up depleted, discouraged, and ready to do anything to feel bet-ter—even at the expense of achieving your most important financial goals.

EXERCISE

1. What are the things you need to do to stay physically healthy, and what are the associated costs?
    - Health insurance: _____ per year
    - Estimated out-of-pocket costs for prescription drugs and necessary medical procedures: _____ per year
    - Preventive activities like working out at the gym, eating healthy, taking vitamins, etc.: _____ per year
    - Other: _____ per year

2. If you are financially struggling, are there ways to get discounts or alternative ways to get similar benefits free of charge? For example, walking or running instead of going to the gym where you'd need to buy a membership; or finding lower-cost prescription drugs by going to a different pharmacy or choosing the generic option to save money. _____

3. How much money can you save by taking advantage of these resources? _____

4. What do you need to do to take care of your mental health, and what are the associated costs?
   - Yoga, meditation, and other things that help you keep perspective _____
   - Therapy _____
   - Time off work (which may impact income if you work part-time) _____
   - Other _____

5. If you are financially struggling, where can you save money using employer resources or finding creative ways to get the benefits you need, e.g., speaking to a pastor instead of a therapist, using breaks and paid time off instead of unpaid time off work.

6. What is the total when you add up everything listed?
   - Total if you are not financially struggling: _____
   - Total if you are financially struggling: _____

Note

If you are in a financial crisis, you will need to limit your self-care to making sure you have healthcare coverage for yourself and any dependents and tapping into employer or community resources to find ways to stay as physically and mentally healthy as possible.

11

ENVISION THE LIFE YOU WANT

Now that you have your financial self-care plan in place, it's time to focus on the future so you can create the life you've always wanted for yourself and your family. When we ask employees about their vision for their future, there are typically three responses:

1. **Some people have an incredibly detailed vision that includes a combination of "must-have" financial and life goals.** This is most common with those under 30, who often have a clear idea of everything they want to accomplish in life, along with a timetable for each milestone—from buying a car, to traveling, getting married, buying a home, having children, and becoming financially independent. They even have a clear vision for which kind of car, where to travel, what type of person they want to marry, what their dream home will be, how many children they want to have, and when they expect to be financially independent so they can live on their own terms, which usually means enjoying the dream life they built through the previous steps without having the pressures that come with earning a paycheck.

2. **Others are on the opposite end of the spectrum.** They know what they don't want from tough experiences they faced, and they know emotionally how they want to feel about their life—for example, being totally free from financial stress, being able to really enjoy the present free of worries or distraction, and having deep, meaningful relationships that bring them joy. But beyond that, they don't have a clear idea of their financial goals.

3. **How most of us operate when it comes to envisioning our future is somewhere in the middle.** We have our "nonnegotiables"—those things we feel we must have to be happy in life, for instance, a life partner, an amazing career, children, a home of our own, the ability to travel the world someday, or any number of other things that we feel are integral to our vision of a happy life, without a "master plan" of specific time frames.

Each approach has its pros and cons. If you have everything "planned out," you will likely discover that life doesn't always happen how we've planned, and often the things you didn't expect that initially serve to derail your plans end up being your greatest blessings. You will likely also discover that what you want changes over time. (This applies as well to people who have nonnegotiables.)

If, on the other hand, your vision is too abstract, you may have a hard time achieving it because you haven't taken the time to really think through your most important priorities—and, you don't have enough of a starting point to even set tangible financial goals, let alone achieve them.

So how do you create a vision for your ideal life that is (1) clear enough to serve as the basis for your plan and (2) flexible enough to manage priorities that may change over time, as well as support your financial goals that will change accordingly?

The answer is to create a clear vision based on where you are today and plan accordingly, but revisit your vision at regular time intervals (our team of coaches recommend annually) to make sure it is still aligned with what you want.

Here's the process we use with the people we coach to do just that:

1. **Identify what you really care about.** And conversely, identify
    what you may have thought was important but actually
    doesn't make you happy. These are often things we have been
    conditioned to think are critical to having a happy life but
    don't actually make us personally happy. For example, maybe
    the "white picket fence" life is not what you truly want; it's
    simply what you've been told all your life is something you
    should aspire to. As we coach people through this part of the
    process, we often hear them say, "I want [insert goal here],"
    and then reveal that when they really think about it, that's not
    what they want at all. This happens quite often with buying a
    home. For most people, buying a home has become inextricably
    intertwined with the concept of the American dream—a key
    life milestone that people covet because it makes them feel like
    they've crossed an important threshold of adulthood, especially
    if children are involved. However, often when we coach people
    who are bound and determined to buy a home, we discover
    that not only is it not in their best interest financially because
    they can't afford the down payment or mortgage based on their
    savings and salary, but it isn't actually what they want. The
    same people that talk about buying a home often later bring
    up the importance of flexibility and their desire to travel and
    experience life in different places! They don't want to be tied
    down to a single location for a long period of time, which is
    when buying a home makes the most sense, nor do they want
    the responsibilities associated with being their own landlord.

    If this sounds remotely like you (either this goal in
    particular or other goals that you have been conditioned to
    aspire to), as you build your vision for your dream life, you need
    to let go of what everyone else says you should want, and tune
    into what you actually want. After all, you are the one who has
    to live your life and live with the consequences of the choices
    you make.

2. **Prioritize by determining what you feel is essential to have** in order to create the life you want (your must-have goals) and what you'd like to have but can live happily without if need be (your "nice-to-have" goals). This will give you a framework to begin identifying your most important financial goals so you can work toward achieving those first. You can always achieve nice-to-have goals after you've accomplished the things that matter most to you, but it's important to differentiate between the foundational goals that you feel are absolutely integral to a meaningful live and the nice-to-have "enhancements"—the cherry on top, so to speak. Table 7.1 will help you do just that.

TABLE 7.1 Taking Stock

What You Envision for Your Life	Already Have	Don't Want	Nice to Have	Must Have
Having a life partner				
Getting married to your life partner				
Having your own car				
Buying your dream home				
Starting your own business				
Having children				
Providing for a college education for your children (if you have them)				
Getting additional education for yourself				
Taking care of parents or other family members as needed				
Achieving financial independence as early as possible				
Creating a legacy				

To see how this plays out in real life, here's an example.

TANYA'S STORY

Tanya, an employee we coached, had just gone through a divorce. She was looking to reevaluate what she wanted from life and to plan accordingly. Tanya grew up in a typical middle-class suburb in New Jersey, with parents who had a long, relatively strong marriage, and she had a traditional Catholic upbringing. Her parents were Italian immigrants, who taught her the importance of family; they raised her with the expectation that she would marry a nice Italian man, have several children, and become a devoted mother. They saw her intelligence and potential (she ultimately became a computer programmer, which her parents supported), and they did encourage her to "use that big brain." But there was never a question that marriage and motherhood were paramount. Everything else was "extra."

It turns out that motherhood was not in her future, even after years of going through in vitro fertilization (IVF), and this caused her marriage to break down. At the same time, Tanya had a revelation—she didn't actually want children. Her parents wanted grandchildren, and her ex-husband wanted a "football team" of boys. But when she really thought about it, her first reaction to each failed IVF attempt was relief! As much as she loved her nieces and nephews, she didn't want children of her own.

Underneath the analytical computer programmer was a free spirit who wanted to be able to pack her bags and travel or even relocate to experience different areas of the country and the world. Financial freedom was important because she had a million interests and hobbies and wanted to be able to pursue them outside of work, including potentially starting her own business or foundation one day to support women who wanted to have careers in technology. After her failed marriage, and all the financial and emotional challenges that came with the divorce, she decided that she never wanted to get married again. But she did want a life partner who had similar values and aspirations, and she did envision living with this person and combining finances, because she wanted that feeling of building a great life with someone she loved—a person who would stand by her side but also give her the freedom to be herself. Lots to unpack there, but we did it, step by step. Table 7.2 shows what her decisions looked like.

TABLE 7.2   Tanya Takes Stock

What You Envision for Your Life	Already Have	Don't Want	Nice to Have	Must Have
Having a life partner			X (She wanted a life partner but was happy on her own)	
Getting married to your life partner		X		
Having your own car	X			
Buying your dream home	X			
Starting your own business			X	
Having children		X		
Providing for a college education for your children (if you have them)		X		
Getting additional education for yourself			X	
Taking care of parents or other family members as needed				X (Her parents didn't have a lot of money, and it was deeply important to her to make sure they were well taken care of the rest of their lives, with best-in-class healthcare being a top priority)

Achieving financial independence as early as possible				X (Since she knew her life would evolve, she wanted to make sure she achieved financial independence as early as possible so she had the flexibility to do whatever she wanted without having to worry about money)
Creating a legacy				X (As she dug deep into what she truly wanted, she realized that her passion to support women who wanted to have careers in computer programming was more of a calling, and that legacy was incredibly important to her)

After clarifying her goals, Tanya was able to significantly increase her savings (made possible by her considerable income and the money she was able to save from not having to continue IVF) and create an investment strategy designed around her must-have goals.

As of the writing of this book, she has achieved all her must-have goals, and she is now thinking through her nice-to-have goals, with her first priority being attending graduate school to get her MBA—something she always wanted but put on the back burner as she focused on her marriage and IVF treatments. She was surprised to discover that she qualified for full tuition reimbursement from her employer, provided she agreed to stay with the company for a minimum of five years. She is going to revisit starting her own company—a tutoring service to help young women learn computer programming—after she has her MBA and has fulfilled her obligation to her employer for her tuition reimbursement.

12

PLANNING FOR KEY LIFE GOALS

Now that you've identified your most important life goals, you need to plan for them. Planning for goals is not easy, because it's a process where first you have to figure out how much you will need to save or invest to achieve your goals in your desired time frame, and then you have to determine if that is actually realistic for your budget. In our experience at Financial Finesse, most people end up having to make changes to their original plans because the amount they would need to save to achieve all their goals, within the time frames they originally set, would require too much of a financial sacrifice—forcing them to cut expenses that dramatically change their lifestyle or compromise their financial self-care, which is critical to being able to sustain financial progress.

That said, it's best to start with the ideal plan in mind, because your vision should always lead your planning; otherwise, you essentially give up on what you really want before you even start. As a first step, we typically recommend writing down each goal, the time frame in which you want to achieve it, and the amount of money it will take to achieve it (understanding you should factor in an inflation rate of about 3 percent annually when you set the cost of each goal unless it's a short term goal you want to reach in a couple of years, in which case, using the current inflation rate is best).

Then plug all that information into an online calculator to determine how much you need to save on a monthly basis to achieve your goal. Figure 12.1 shows what this looks like. You can access our Saving for Goals calculator at www.ffcalcs.com/save_for_goals.

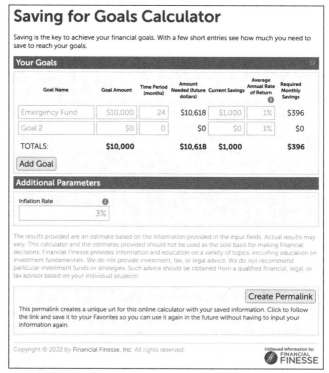

FIGURE 12.1   This calculator will let you determine how much money you will need to save to achieve your goals.

Please note that as you input your goals into the calculator, you'll be prompted to enter a rate of return on the money you save or invest for each goal. Here's some guidance on how to determine the best rate of return to use based on the time frame for each goal:

- **For goals that you want to achieve in 5 years** (60 months) or less, you'll want to input a very low rate of return into the goals calculator—around 1 to 2 percent—because this money will need to be kept in an account that earns only a minimal amount of interest, like a money market, CD, or savings account, where you can tap into it whenever you need to.

- **For goals that are 5 to 10 years away** (61 to 120 months), you'll want to input a moderate rate of return, because you can afford to take a little bit more risk with these goals, investing a portion in the stock market, a portion in bonds, and a portion in cash. A 5 to 6 percent return is reasonable in this scenario.

- **For goals that are more than 10 years** (120 months) away, you can take more risk for a higher return. It's reasonable to input an 8 to 9 percent return into the calculator for this scenario if you are investing a larger percentage of your portfolio in the stock market, ideally through low-cost equity mutual funds.

After you utilize the goals calculator, one of two things will happen: Either you'll look at the total monthly amount you need to save and realize that it's simply too much to sacrifice for your current budget, in which case you will need to make changes by delaying the goals that aren't time sensitive or by changing the scale of the goal to reduce how much you need to save. Or you'll be pleasantly surprised to discover that your plan is doable based on your budget, in which case you can begin planning for the specific goals you are looking to achieve.

Once you have your must-have goals in place, along with a plan to save for them based on what works with your budget, it's time to focus on the steps you need to take to reach your must-have goals. This chapter takes you through many of the different goals listed in Chapter 11, so you have a road map showing exactly what you need to do to achieve each goal.

BUYING A CAR

The first big purchase that most of us make is a car. It can also be your first big financial win or mistake. Let's take a look at some steps to take:

- **Define your goals.** Start by thinking about your needs and the type of vehicle that would fit them. (There are no right or wrong answers here as long as you're being honest with yourself.)

Do you just need something to get you back and forth from school or work? How many passengers might you have? Do you need something rugged for the area you'll be driving in? Do you want a brand-new car, or are you OK driving something used? How far and often will you be driving it?

■ **Figure out the most cost-effective way of achieving your goals.** Don't just look at the sticker price when comparison shopping among various vehicles and deciding whether to lease or buy. Sites for Edmunds and Kelley Blue Book offer a "true cost to own" analysis of various cars over a period of time that includes things like depreciation, interest rates on a car loan, taxes, fees, insurance premiums, gas, maintenance and repairs, and any federal tax credits that may be available. You may be surprised how a cheap car that depreciates quickly and/or is not fuel efficient and needs repairs can end up costing more in the long run than a more expensive car.

In general, the most cost-effective approach in the long run is to purchase a good used car and keep it for as long as possible. Just be sure to have your mechanic look over any used car before you buy it so you don't get stuck with any surprise repair bills. On the other hand, if you have the money to do so without compromising your most important financial goals, and you really want a brand-new car every two to three years, you're probably better off leasing as long as you stay within the mileage requirements.

■ **Understand the trade-offs.** Once you've estimated the total cost of your vehicle (including insurance, gas, maintenance, and repairs), see how it fits into your budget. If it's more than what you've allocated, ask yourself what you're willing to sacrifice to afford the car or if you'd prefer to buy something less expensive.

BUYING A HOME

As we discussed in the previous chapter, buying a home is not necessarily a financial goal that makes sense for everyone, but for people who plan to live in the same place for a long period of time, it's often the next major financial goal after buying a car. Below are the steps to take if buying a home is one of your financial goals:

- **Take steps to improve and protect your credit.** While having good credit is important in qualifying for a car loan or lease, it's even more crucial when getting a mortgage, because even a small difference in interest rates can add up to quite a bit over the life of the mortgage. For example, say average interest rates for a 30-year mortgage vary between about 5 and 7 percent, depending on your credit score—the higher your score, the lower your rate. In this scenario, if you look at a $480,000 30-year mortgage, the difference between having excellent credit (where you qualify for the 5 percent rate) and fair credit (where you qualify for the 7 percent rate) is over $220,000 over the life of the mortgage. That's the difference your credit score can make!

  The first thing you can do is check your credit reports for errors. It's been estimated that about one in three people have errors on their credit reports that could be hurting their scores. It's bad enough to pay for your own mistakes. You don't want to pay for someone else's. You can get a free copy of each of your credit reports (Experian, Equifax, and TransUnion) every 12 months at annualcreditreport.com and dispute any errors you may find.

  If you have any delinquent debts, try to pay them off in full or at least settle them, starting with the most recent ones. Old debts fall off your credit reports after seven years, but you may still be sued for them depending on the statute of limitations in your state. Be aware that acknowledging the debt can restart that clock. To avoid future missed payments, consider setting your debt payments so they are paid automatically.

Paying down debts you're not delinquent on can also improve your credit score as well as your debt-to-income ratio. Just be careful about closing credit cards as you pay them off, especially ones you've had a long time, because that can reduce your credit history and increase your credit utilization (debt balances divided by your credit limit) if you still have any remaining debt. If you're worried about running the credit card balance up again, you can destroy the card or make it hard to use without closing it. You may also be able to convert fee cards to no-fee cards.

Even if your credit score is stellar (760 and above should get you the best mortgage rates), you may want to take some steps to keep it that way. Placing a security freeze on your credit reports can prevent an identity thief from opening credit in your name. Companies like Experian and Credit Karma (which covers the other two credit bureaus) offer free credit monitoring that can alert you if anything does happen to your credit so you can clean it up before more damage is done.

- **Save for the down payment and closing costs.** Unless you qualify for a VA loan, you may want to try to put down 20 percent to avoid paying private mortgage insurance (PMI). You'll probably also have to pay closing costs of about 2 to 3 percent of the home's purchase price plus whatever you spend on moving, furniture, and improvements. This can add up to a lot of money, so the sooner you can start saving, the better. (In addition to regular savings and family gifts or loans, you can withdraw up to $10,000 from an IRA penalty-free for a first-time home purchase, and many employer retirement plans allow you to borrow from them, often with a longer repayment period if the money is used to purchase your principal residence.)

- **Put together your real estate team.** Once your credit and savings are ready, it's time to find the professionals who will help you with next steps. That usually begins with a real estate agent who can help you select and manage the rest of the team. Ask people you know for referrals for an agent who ideally has experience in the neighborhood(s) and with the type of home you're interested in.

Your real estate agent can then refer you to mortgage brokers/loan officers, a real estate attorney, and possibly a title agent, depending on your state. While it may be tempting to choose a mortgage company purely based on price, a mortgage officer with a good working relationship with your real estate agent can be very helpful. The one professional you may want to select independent of your real estate agent is a home inspector, who might otherwise be incentivized to look past problems in your home to help the agent close the deal.

■ **Get preapproved for the right mortgage.** Preapproval is much more than just prequalification since it means you have a commitment from the loan company. This gives you a leg up against other buyers in a competitive market, and some real estate agents even require it before showing you homes.

When choosing a mortgage, consider how much you can afford to pay a month and how long you plan to keep the home. A 30-year mortgage tends to have a lower monthly payment than a 15-year mortgage, but you'll pay more in interest. Be careful of mortgages whose interest rates are adjustable, because the payment can jump significantly if the rate goes up. A good rule of thumb is to have the rate fixed for as long as you intend to keep the home. Finally, try to do all your rate shopping within two weeks so the credit inquiries count as one on your credit report.

Remember that just because a mortgage company will make you a loan doesn't mean you can really afford it. Once you get a calculation of the mortgage payment (including estimated taxes and insurance), make sure it fits into your budget. If not, look for expenses to cut, or target less expensive homes.

Once you have this foundation in place (pun intended), the fun part of shopping for the home begins. Your real estate agent should be able to walk you through this and the rest of the process. Just be sure to restrict your search to homes that fall within your budget before you see something that tempts you to bust that budget!

GETTING MARRIED (OR NOT)

First of all, should you get married to your life partner? There are financial pros and cons either way. The main financial benefits are that you and your spouse can bypass gift and estate taxes for any money that you decide to give or pass on to one another, access many of each other's employee benefits, make spousal IRA contributions, easily buy a home together, receive spousal Social Security benefits, be each other's default beneficiaries, and stretch out distributions from an inherited IRA. The main financial benefits of not getting married are being able to contribute to a family and an individual HSA, possibly saving money on income-based student loan repayment plans, having your own SALT (state and local tax) deductions, filing as single and head of household if one of you has children for a higher total standard deduction, and, of course, avoiding the potential of an expensive divorce (which you can also do with a good prenuptial agreement).

- **Start planning and saving for the wedding and honeymoon.** The average cost of a wedding is around $20,000, and another $5,000 on average for the honeymoon. Of course, that's average. Yours might be a lot more or a lot less, so start thinking about the type of wedding and honeymoon you want and what the costs would be. Then divide that amount by the number of months before your wedding, and have that amount automatically transferred to a separate savings account.
- **Have the "money talk."** Find a time for you and your partner to talk about how you want to handle your finances. Realize that conflicts about money are usually really about deeper values.

Read the sections of this book together about your money scripts and financial identities as well as your must-haves and nice-to-haves.

- **Decide whether to handle finances together or separately.** Setting up joint bank and credit card accounts can simplify handling household expenses and make you feel more like a couple. If one of you has a poor credit score, being added to the other's credit cards can help improve the "added" spouse's score. The money in the bank accounts is also immediately available to your spouse should something happen to you, and vice versa.

    However, there are some downsides to combining finances. These include potentially fighting more about how to spend money, or worse, discovering your spouse has used your joint account to make large purchases you didn't agree upon beforehand, your spouse's debts becoming your own, and a lack of privacy when one of you wants to give a surprise gift to the other.

    One option is to have one or more joint accounts for household bills and savings and separate accounts for personal expenses. Most states allow you to set up your individual bank account with a POD, or payable on death, registration that allows the account to pass directly to your beneficiary without going through the time and expense of probate. To help you manage your joint accounts, you can both use an app like Mint to monitor household expenses and withdrawals.

- **Know your credit scores.** Your credit scores don't merge when you get married, but if you apply for joint loans like a mortgage, the person with the lower credit score can have a negative impact on the interest rate or chance of qualifying at all. Be sure you know your credit scores before applying for any joint loans, and take steps to improve and protect both of your scores.

- **Update your estate planning.** It's never too early to create or update your wills, durable powers of attorney, and healthcare directives. You'll also want to update the beneficiary information on any retirement accounts, life insurance policies, and trusts you may have. This is especially true if they still list an ex-spouse since the beneficiary registration generally trumps whatever you say in a will. Once you're married, having your spouse as the beneficiary on your retirement accounts also gives your spouse the unique ability to roll the account(s) into his or her own IRA, allowing your spouse to potentially benefit longer from tax deferral.

HAVING A BABY

Having a child can be one of the most significant things we ever do. It almost seems wrong to think about money as a factor at all. However, being money strong can go a long way in reducing the financial stress of parenthood (which can be stressful enough on its own). Here are some costs you may want to prepare for:

- **Childbirth.** The most important thing you can do here is to make sure that you have health insurance that covers childbirth since the procedure can cost tens of thousands of dollars. Fortunately, out-of-pocket costs for people with health insurance typically average around $3,000, but that's still an expense you'll want to be prepared for. See if your employer offers a supplemental healthcare policy that provides cash in the event of a hospital stay since that's one of the only hospital stays you can know of in advance. You can also contribute what you may spend on childbirth pretax to an HSA or healthcare FSA, depending on which one you're eligible for, and use the money tax-free for your out-of-pocket costs.
- **Baby furniture and other big expenses.** Make a list of items you'll need, and start researching the costs. You can plan to spend less by purchasing used items, as long as you make sure the items are up to code.

  Don't forget the cost of updating your will and/or trust. (Without an updated will, the court will decide who will raise your child should something happen to you.) Your employer may offer you free or discounted access to basic legal documents through an employee assistance program or other employee benefit. If you want to hire an attorney, see if you can sign up for a prepaid legal plan during your annual benefits enrollment so you can get discounted or free legal services. You can always choose not to renew the plan after your documents are updated.

Once you have a target amount in mind, divide that number by the number of months you have to save. Then have that amount automatically transferred from your checking to a savings account each month for this purpose. Making that space in your budget for savings will also help you afford the following expenses once you have the baby.

- **Childcare.** Find out what the maternity/paternity leave policies are at both your and your partner's place of employment, so you can estimate how long you'll each be available to provide full-time care. Keep in mind that you'll need to have enough savings to replace your income(s) if the leave isn't paid. If you both return to work, you'll need childcare, so find out what the costs of childcare are in your area. (Infant daycare can average between $6,000 and $23,000 a year depending on where you live, while a full-time nanny averages about $29,000 a year.) For those who don't have parents who are able or willing to take on childcare responsibilities (which can be a big ask), many employers offer dependent care flexible spending accounts that allow you to contribute money pretax for childcare expenses. This reduces your taxable income and can save you up to 30 percent or more depending on your tax bracket.
- **Other ongoing expenses.** A USDA study found that average middle-class American families spend about $13,000 on their child per year. Some of those costs may be offset by spending less on entertainment, travel, dining out, and other leisure activities that you'll have less time for. (You do know that will happen, don't you?) You'll have to make room for the rest in

your budget, so you may want to start thinking about how you'll do that now.

PROVIDING FUNDING FOR EDUCATION

Whether for yourself, your children, or your grandchildren, funding education expenses is one of the most common financial goals. With college costs rising so much faster than inflation, education is also one of the most difficult to fund. Here are some steps to take:

- **Make sure you're saving enough for your retirement goals first.** It can be tempting to prioritize your children's education, but there's no financial aid for retirement. One of the best gifts you can give your children is role modeling good financial planning and not be a financial burden on them in your later years.

- **Set an education funding goal.** Very few people are able to fully fund four years at a private college. One option might be to try to save enough to cover in-state public education, a school within commuting distance, or two years at a community college followed by two years at a four-year school. If the students make other choices, they can cover the difference with financial aid. If that's still not doable, you can use the net price calculator on college websites to estimate how much the school will expect you to pay out of pocket.

- **Calculate how much to save.** You can use a calculator on sites like savingforcollege.com to estimate how much to save to reach your goal. You can then have that amount automatically transferred to a savings account earmarked for education.

- **Decide where your savings will go.** Many people's first instinct is to open an account in their child's name, but that has some drawbacks. The money is the child's so it has to be used for the child's benefit, but any income over $2,200 per year is taxed at your tax rate. The money has a greater impact on financial aid than your assets, and once your child reaches the age of majority in your state, your child can use the money however she or he likes.

The most popular option is a 529 college savings plan. Each state offers its own plans with different investment options. You're not limited to the plan(s) in your state. If you live in a state with an income tax, you may get a state tax deduction or credit for contributing to a 529 plan (usually this must be your own state's plan). The main benefit is that you don't have to pay taxes on the investment earnings if you use the money for qualified education expenses. There is, however, a tax penalty if you use the money for something else.

The 529 prepaid plans differ from savings plans in that with a prepaid plan you're buying units, credits, or numbers of years of tuition at participating schools for the future education expenses of a student beneficiary. Just be sure to read the fine print to understand what happens if the student goes to a different school. In that case, many plans only credit you a low interest rate on the money.

■ **Look for ways to reduce costs.** If you're not able to save enough to cover all the education costs, there are still things you can do to save money. While your children are still in high school, they can take AP classes to earn college credits that may allow them to graduate college early. You can search for scholarships they may qualify for. They may also want to consider choosing a school that gives them a scholarship or grant even if it's lower ranked since there is limited evidence showing that going to higher-ranked schools actually will result in higher lifetime income except for a few fields like consulting and investment banking.

■ **Check out your employee benefits for help.** If you're funding your own education, your employer may help you. Many have tuition reimbursement programs that you may qualify for. Some also have student loan repayment programs that can lessen the burdens of any student loans you take.

STARTING YOUR OWN BUSINESS

Are you dreaming of starting a business? If so, you don't want to neglect your own personal finances. I can tell you from firsthand experience that having a strong foundation for your personal finances is key.

- **Build up a bigger emergency fund.** Since most businesses fail because of cash flow problems, you may want to build up enough emergency savings to cover your own necessary expenses for at least 9 to 12 months or however long your business plan projects it will take to earn enough income to pay your bills. Otherwise, you may be forced to abandon your dream business during a rough patch before it has a chance to succeed. Keep in mind that those savings are to cover your essential living expenses and should be in addition to money you need to cover business costs.

- **Get your credit in shape.** You'll also want to ideally get your credit score to 750 or above if you'll be applying for business loans. If you need to improve your credit score, take the credit management steps we discussed earlier in the section on buying a home. That includes paying down any high interest debt you may have, which also improves your debt-to-income ratio.

- **Put together your team.** That includes a good business lawyer to advise you on business structure and any permits, licenses, contracts, zoning rules, and other regulatory requirements your business will need to satisfy. A CPA can help you with accounting and taxes. An insurance agent or broker can help you replace the insurance benefits you would normally get as an employee (primarily health, disability, and life insurance), and help you assess the insurance needs of the business itself. If you expect to make a profit, you may also want to speak with a financial advisor about setting up a retirement plan for yourself and your employees.

CARING FOR ELDERLY PARENTS

It's not just the kids that you have to plan for. As life spans increase, people are increasingly taking care of their aging parents as well. This can be difficult, both emotionally and financially. Here are some steps you can take to make the process easier:

- **Determine if your parents need help.** Is their home increasingly in disrepair? Is their health deteriorating? Are there signs of cognitive impairment? These may all be indicators that they need help. If your parents are uncooperative, you may want to get the assistance of an aging life care professional.

- **Gather as much important information as you can.** Get any contact information, legal documents, medical records, and financial information. Your parents may want to draft or update a durable power of attorney, HIPAA authorization, advance healthcare directive, and will/trust while they can.

- **Figure out the best place for them to live.** If they're healthy and can function well on their own, an independent living facility can be an option. If they have health issues that require monitoring and help with daily living, an assisted-living facility may be preferable. They can also choose to have a caregiver come to their home. However, they may need a nursing home if they have a progressive condition that requires extensive care.

- **Figure out how they will pay for care.** Some senior facilities are private pay only, and some are income-based. If they have a long-term care insurance policy, you'll want to see what it covers. Check any life insurance policies and annuities they may have for long-term care riders. If their resources are limited, contact your local department of aging ombudsman program, council on aging, or area agency on aging for guidance.

- **Make a plan for you to be the caregiver.** You may want to draft a personal care agreement between you and your parent(s). If you'll be providing care yourself, find out what your employer's leave policy is and whether you can make arrangements for working flex time or working from home. Your employer may offer an employee assistance program with resources. If you need to take time off work, plan for any loss of income and benefits.

PLANNING FOR FINANCIAL INDEPENDENCE

This is probably the most common goal of the people we work with. Financial independence is a big part of what being money strong is all about. It's having the freedom to do what you want on your terms. It's not all or nothing though. Think of it as a series of stages.

- **Start with an emergency fund.** Having an emergency fund is what allows you to walk away from a bad job situation or survive a layoff. Financial planners typically recommend you have enough savings to cover your living expenses for at least three to six months so you can keep a roof over your head, food on the table, your car in the garage, and the lights on while you're in between jobs. That may seem overwhelming at first though, so set a more immediate goal of $1,000, and then progressively build from there to get to your ultimate emergency savings goal.

- **Set a long-term goal for financial independence.** Think about how much income you'd need if you didn't have to work anymore. You typically need about 70 to 80 percent of your current income since you won't be saving for retirement and you may have debts like a mortgage, student loans, etc., that would be paid off. You may also plan to downsize or move to an area with a lower cost of living. On the other hand, you may need more income if you'll be enjoying a lot of travel and other expensive hobbies, so it all depends on your situation and goals.

- **Calculate how much to save.** This sounds complicated, but there are a number of free online calculators that make it relatively simple, including our own at ffcalcs.com/retirement_ estimator. Don't get too hung up on the exact numbers though. There are a lot of assumptions that are bound to change over time. The idea is to make sure you're in the ballpark and then continue updating and adjusting your savings rate accordingly.

■ **Decide where to put your savings.** Here's a general framework to follow, understanding you should consult with a financial coach or financial planner for guidance on your specific situation:

- **Step 1:** If your employer matches your employer sponsored retirement plan contributions up to a certain amount, you'll want to start by contributing enough to capture that full match so you don't leave "free money" on the table.

- **Step 2:** If you have a high-deductible health insurance plan that's eligible for an HSA (health savings account), contribute to your HSA since the money goes in pretax and can come out tax-free for qualified healthcare expenses or at least penalty-free for anything once you turn 65.

- **Step 3:** Once you max out your HSA, we recommend you return to funding your retirement plan and contribute up to the maximum allowed into the plan. While your employer sponsored retirement plan doesn't have as many tax advantages as the HSA, it is still an excellent vehicle for shielding your money from taxes, because you don't have to pay any taxes until you make withdrawals when you retire.

- **Step 4:** After you've done all of the above, if you have extra money you want to invest, we recommend considering an IRA, which has tax advantages. Just beware that the mutual funds you choose to invest in within your IRA may have higher fees than those in your employer's retirement plan, especially if you work for a large employer who can negotiate very favorable fees from mutual fund companies. This is why we typically recommend maxing out your employer's retirement plan before opening an IRA.

- **Step 5:** If you want to save more than what you can contribute to these tax-advantaged accounts, the last step is to invest in a regular taxable account.

■ **Consider investing in low-cost target date funds.** The easiest way to invest your retirement savings is to put everything into a target date fund with the year closest to when you plan to retire and leave it alone. These funds are designed to be fully diversified "one-stop shops" that automatically get more conservative as you approach the target retirement date so you can "set it and forget it." If you have a choice of target date funds, look for ones that are made up of low-cost index funds or at least have low expense ratios. Studies have found low fees to be a good predictor of a fund's performance relative to similar investments.

PLANNING YOUR LEGACY

Once you've accomplished your personal goals, what's next? Leaving a legacy is about what you pass on to others. While this is a complex topic that should be addressed with a good estate planning attorney, here are some things to consider:

■ **Define your legacy.** What is most important to you? Are there particular people or causes you'd like to support after you pass away?

■ **Minimize estate taxes and probate costs.** Regardless of where you want your assets to go, it's probably not to Uncle Sam or legal fees. Fortunately, you can pass up to a total of $12.06 million without estate and gift taxes in 2022. If you're married, you and your spouse can each use your combined exemptions.

If you're still concerned about having a taxable estate, you'll want to consult with a qualified estate planning attorney about how trusts can be used to reduce your estate tax liability. For example, you can use a charitable remainder trust to donate to charity while getting a charitable deduction and removing assets from your estate. If you can't avoid the liability, consider purchasing life insurance to pay the taxes if you're concerned about your heirs having to sell a business or real estate to pay the estate taxes.

The more common obstacle that people face when passing on their assets is the time and cost of probate, which is when the court processes your estate. This can cost thousands of dollars in legal fees and take months or even years of time if there's litigation. You can easily bypass probate by having a living beneficiary designated to receive your assets when you pass. In addition to qualified accounts, life insurance, and annuities, you can add beneficiaries to a bank account with a POD form, to a regular investment account with a TOD (transfer on death) form and, in some states, to real estate and vehicles. A revocable living trust is often used to add beneficiaries to assets that you otherwise couldn't.

- **Decide if you want to attach "strings" to your estate.** A trust can also be used to appoint someone to manage the trust assets for a period of time or until a specified event occurs. This is particularly useful when you're passing assets to a minor or to a person with special needs, and you can even use it for the purpose of taking care of a pet. A trust allows you to designate how the assets are managed, by whom, and for how long.

- **Don't forget the intangibles.** You probably don't want your legacy to just be about wealth. Some people create an informal "ethical will" that passes on things like family stories, lessons, and even an explanation of terms in a will or trust that may be confusing or hurtful. This isn't a legal document and can even be in the form of a video.

Module 4

ROLE MODEL GOOD FINANCIAL HABITS AND BEHAVIORS

ABOUT THIS MODULE

Now that you have a plan to attain the life you want, it's time to turn your attention to the fourth step in the START™ framework—role modeling good financial habits and behaviors for others. This may seem counterintuitive. Most people feel like they have enough to do just managing their own finances, and their first response is that they don't have the time, energy, or knowledge to role model with intention—meaning proactively sharing what they've learned with others who are going through similar financial challenges.

But what they are missing with this response is that intentionally role modeling is actually one of the best things they can do for their own finances. Most of the formal studies on role modeling focus on the benefit to the recipient, such as how much mentorship can benefit those who receive it. But more recently a new body of research has found that taking the step of actually helping others is one of the most impactful things you can do to continue your own success. And this tracks with our experience working with millions of people to improve their finances. We've worked with thousands of people to help them become intentional financial role models, and in virtually every single instance they've accelerated their own financial progress as a result of the experience.

Why? Because when you are in a position to set the example for others, you are operating at the highest level of accountability, beyond even what a coach can provide. You make even better financial decisions knowing that how you manage your finances will have a ripple effect on others—and that creates a snowball effect where your financial progress accelerates at a faster rate than those who choose not to intentionally role model others.

If you are thinking, "Ok, I get that, but how on earth am I supposed to be a role model when I bought this book because I need help figuring out this whole financial thing?" you are not alone. In fact, our coaches encounter this reaction all the time when they broach the topic of role modeling.

The term "role model" itself can be daunting. Even people who have achieved great financial success typically don't see themselves as financial role models. They get stuck in all the financial challenges they had along the way or the areas they still need to work on. They think they are not ready to be a role model, because in their minds, a financial role model is the epitome of financial perfection.

If you too are thinking this way, you are thinking of the "role model" in a way that is much different than how we (and the dictionary) define it—and that is probably where the disconnect lies.

The dictionary definition of a role model is "a person who is looked to by others as an example to be imitated." Given that nearly 70 percent of employees are struggling financially, to the extent you have been able to overcome your own financial challenges—or make significant progress toward that end either before you picked up this book or as a result of actions you've taken as a result of reading the previous modules—you are, in fact, someone who provides an example for others to imitate to achieve their own financial success. In other words, you are already a role model whether you like it or not!

The decision you have to make at this point is whether you operate as a passive financial role model (outside of role modeling good financial habits and behaviors for your children, which is a critical component of parenting) or an intentional financial role model. Here's the distinction:

1. A passive role model is what it sounds like—someone who sets an example simply by virtue of the way that person manages money. Because people inherently watch how others behave, you automatically influence those closest to you without even realizing it. They will notice how you manage your money when you make both minor and major purchases—from dining out, to vacationing, to purchasing a car or home—and will see how your life evolves over time as you achieve greater levels of financial freedom. And when they see a positive connection between the former and the latter, they will take note and typically change their behaviors, at least a little, in a positive way as a result. When you are a passive role model, all you need to do is simply live your life, and you'll influence those you know best in a positive way.

2. An intentional role model takes things a step further. People who are intentional role models actively share all they've overcome—their financial challenges—and teach others the lessons they've learned in the process, as opposed to simply living their lives and influencing others by the examples they set when it comes to money.

Please note that, even considering all the benefits, intentional role modeling is not for everyone. Some people decide that there's more downside than upside to taking on this responsibility, and there's nothing wrong with that. Only you can make this determination, and you should make it based on what works best for your life, versus forcing yourself into a situation that doesn't fit with how you want to live your life. If you are an incredibly private person and are uncomfortable sharing your financial story with others, or you feel like you already have too much on your plate to become an intentional role model (and you don't have children who require it), I recommend you skip this module altogether and move on to Chapter 15. Role modeling should not be a punishing activity that drains your energy; it should be something that uplifts you as well as those who you teach. There's no point in pursuing it if you don't feel it will be a positive experience for you. There are plenty of other ways to make an impact on others, and you still have all the other tips and techniques in this book to benefit your own financial situation without having to take on this level of responsibility.

13

INTENTIONAL ROLE MODELING

Since you are reading this chapter, I'm assuming you have decided you want to be an intentional financial role model—essentially sharing how you overcame (or are overcoming) your personal financial challenges and teaching others the lessons you learned—for both the benefits you will receive and the benefits you can provide others.

DETERMINING THE BEST WAY TO INTENTIONALLY ROLE MODEL

The first step in this process is to determine what type of intentional role modeling works best for you, based on your interests, skill sets, and time constraints. We all have different levels of comfort when it comes to sharing our personal stories and the lessons we've learned, as well as different ways of communicating. The key is to focus on the approach that gives you the most personal fulfillment, because that will automatically translate into the best result.

I personally find tremendous fulfillment from sharing with as many people as possible what I've learned from my experiences, most notably my challenges, how I've overcome them, and the advice I have for anyone going through the same thing. It makes me feel like the struggles I went through were worth it; that there is a larger purpose to the mistakes I made, and something that was painful at the time can be turned into a lesson that not only improved my life but can be paid forward to improve the lives of so many others. Others, like some of our financial coaches who eschew conducting group education sessions in order to work exclusively to foster a 1x1 coaching relationship with individual employees, prefer making their impact in a more private way, trading breadth (reaching as many people as possible) for depth (making a much bigger impact on fewer people that they choose to work with in a 1x1 setting). There is no right or wrong answer here; it's all about what works best for you.

There are essentially three types of intentional role modeling to choose from: doing 1x1 mentoring, teaching groups of people, or going big and sharing your story and the lessons you've learned more broadly. All are essentially a form of teaching others by sharing your experiences and your advice based on the lessons you've learned, with a focus on the areas of financial growth that you are most passionate about—often focusing on helping people who have backgrounds and financial challenges that you relate to because they are very similar to your own. The decision you have to make is how you want to do this. Below is more context on each type of intentional role modeling so you can pick the one that resonates most with you and determine the best way to apply it based on what provides you the greatest sense of personal satisfaction.

1x1 Mentoring

Mentoring can be incredibly fulfilling to both the mentor and the mentee. If you have significant expertise in an area that other people are eager to learn about, or even wisdom that comes from life experiences that you want to impart to others going through similar challenges, mentoring may be a good avenue for you to pursue. Keep in mind, it does entail making a deep commitment to the people you mentor, so you will want to make sure you have the time to meet with them on a regular basis— weekly, biweekly, monthly, or quarterly, whatever you decide. Mentoring works best for people who love working 1x1 with others, and who have a high level of emotional intelligence, including patience and active listening skills. People you mentor are not always going to follow your advice, and it can be frustrating when they don't or when they encounter the same challenges over and over because they can't seem to change their behavior even though they desperately want to. You have to know that this is part of the process when you get into it.

JEN'S STORY

Jen discovered she is highly future-oriented—someone who naturally plans and is excellent at that delicate balance of sticking to the plan when needed and adapting when circumstances arise that require a pivot. She also realized that the challenges she originally had with money, before she began the coaching process, stemmed from having poor money influences in her life. Her parents (and extended family) spent above their means regularly, rendering them unable to pay for her education when the time came for her to look into college, and made worse by the fact her parents' relatively high income level disqualified her from financial aid. She subsequently had to take out student loans in her name, which, coupled with the unintentional messages she got about money growing up, set her up for a life of scrambling to make ends meet even though she, as well, earned a relatively high salary. Once she overcame her financial challenges and developed an entirely new money script and financial identity (leveraging her natural planning skills), Jen decided that she wanted to help parents avoid having to go through the challenges she faced. She recognized that her introverted nature didn't lend itself to teaching large groups of people. She felt she'd get much more satisfaction by selectively working with individual people she related to, whom she could cultivate long-term relationships with and see their progress over time—knowing as well that she was also progressing and that a peer-to-peer mentorship structure would also help her most.

Jen now volunteers part-time at her local youth center working individually with parents to teach them the lessons she learned so they can pass them on to their children—and in the process has picked up a few new lessons from the parents she's taught, who took her lessons and built upon them with creative ideas of their own!

Teaching Groups of People (Typically Through Volunteering)

Teaching groups of people is best for people who enjoy speaking in front of groups and have an innate ability to "read the room" and adapt accordingly. It typically requires a greater time commitment than mentoring does, because you will likely need to create some sort of structure around what you are teaching. In addition, you will need to prepare ahead of time for each class you teach so you are as effective as possible. You also will want to make sure you are both passionate about the topic you are teaching and incredibly well versed in it. This will enable you to share accurate information and create a learning environment that is highly engaging, so that those you teach not only retain but act on the information you share.

MARIE'S STORY

Marie never had the chance to develop any real financial habits—good or bad. Her parents sheltered her from their financial troubles, and she went straight from college to getting married to a man who insisted on managing the finances. She had an incredible job in sales and was bringing home well into six figures of compensation annually between her pay and bonus, but she turned all of it over to her husband to manage. She never paid any attention to the process, thinking that, as an accountant, he was well equipped to manage their finances without her involvement. Unfortunately that was not the case.

When the marriage began to fray and Marie filed for divorce, she was shocked to find out that they were deeply in debt with almost no savings, and all that money she earned had been spent on her husband's mistress at the time. Not only did she have to start from ground zero, living with her parents until she was able to amass enough money to get an apartment of her own, but she had to learn how to manage money for the first time, not having any example to follow. After two years of our coaching, she had built a strong financial foundation, and she was able to buy a home and develop a much healthier relationship with a man she would later marry—where they were able to build wealth together.

Marie and her new husband are now the owners of multiple real estate investment properties as well as a strong investment portfolio—with each of them maxing out their 401(k) plans. She loves her job, and works because she wants to, not because she has to, and she has never felt more fulfilled in her life. Marie discovered through this process that she was both incredibly resilient and incredibly passionate about telling her story in an attempt to help other women avoid the mistake she made with her first husband. This, coupled with her extroverted nature, has prompted her to host webcasts and workshops for women so she can share her story and motivate them to take control of their finances.

Going Big and Sharing Your Story and the Lessons You Learned More Broadly

Going big means publicly sharing your story through your own social media, or press that are interested in profiling people who have overcome financial challenges and the lessons they've learned. At Financial Finesse we have an entire podcast devoted to profiling people who have changed their financial lives and want to use their stories to inspire others to do the same. Some of these people take things a step further by becoming major advocates for financial literacy, developing or joining a coalition of like-minded people who are devoted to solving societal problems connected to a lack of financial literacy. This can be everything from lobbying Congress for laws that require or financially incentivize financial literacy in schools or at the workplace to identifying specific populations in need of financial guidance and finding ways to get them connected to the resources they need. The best advocates view their work as a "calling" and are willing to spend time equivalent to a part-time job to do their part to effect change. If you don't have this level of time or passion, mentoring or teaching may be better avenues for you to intentionally role model positive financial habits and behaviors.

J.R.'S STORY

J.R. was a professional athlete who, like most pro athletes, played for a much shorter period of time than he believed he would. As a pro athlete, he never felt like he had a good understanding of how much of the money he earned should be dedicated to spending, saving, and investing. J.R. stated that he remembers thinking, "People save money to have money, but why do I need to save money, when I already have money?" Once J.R.'s career ended abruptly and his income stopped, his reality hit him like a ton of bricks. J.R. had a cash flow crisis. The amount of money he saved didn't give him much runway compared to his expenses. So when J.R.'s football career ended he had to make drastic cuts to his expenses and his lifestyle. That, coupled with the regret that came from what he could have done with the money he earned to set himself up for a lifetime of financial success, lit a fire in him. He became absolutely determined to "figure the money thing out" and sought ways to intentionally educate himself on the best way to recover from his situation—leveraging a combination of our coaching and advice from peers and mentors who were financially stable and were able to show him what was possible if he stuck to his plans. In the process, he discovered he has an incredible ability to learn from others and apply those lessons to his own situation.

J.R. has since formed a coalition of former players and financial experts, including our financial coaches at Financial Finesse, to bring financial education to college athletes who are now eligible to profit from their name, image, and likeness, showing them how to use that money to get a head start in life. As a result of J.R.'s work and advocacy, he brought us an idea that we believe will change the lives of hundreds of thousands of college athletes; and as I write this, we are working together with J.R. and the coalition he developed to launch NIL Long Game, a financial literacy certification program available free to every single college athlete in the country.

HOW INTENTIONAL ROLE MODELING ACCELERATES YOUR OWN FINANCIAL SUCCESS

As I mention in the introduction to this module, intentional role modeling can significantly accelerate your own financial progress. There are two reasons for this:

1. Intentional role modeling provides you with accountability to those you teach, because you feel an obligation to set a positive example for them, layered on top of the commitment you've already made to yourself. Going back to the first chapter, this is why those who sponsor recovering alcoholics have a much higher success rate of staying sober than those who simply participate in the program—sponsors feel a deep sense of obligation to set the right example.

2. You actually retain information you learn at a much deeper level when you teach it to someone else. This is based on a scientific phenomenon called the "protégé effect"—which uses teaching others as a form of reinforcing what you've learned. Figure 13.1 shows just how impactful teaching others can be on your own learning.

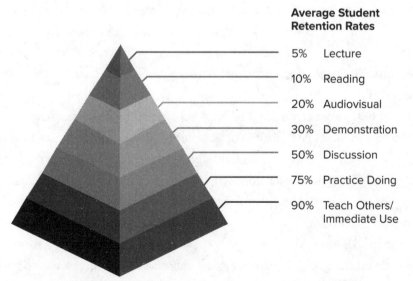

Average Student Retention Rates

5%	Lecture
10%	Reading
20%	Audiovisual
30%	Demonstration
50%	Discussion
75%	Practice Doing
90%	Teach Others/ Immediate Use

FIGURE 13.1   How people learn. (This pyramid model was developed by the National Training Laboratories Institute.)

THE INCREDIBLE IMPACT YOU CAN MAKE THROUGH INTENTIONAL ROLE MODELING

Now I'd like to share how role modeling benefits others, because most people tend to dramatically underestimate the level of impact they can make as an intentional role model, and that impact in and of itself can be incredibly satisfying. In fact, sometimes people who have worked with our financial coaches will subsequently choose to intentionally role model others, and ultimately they will decide to change careers and do the hard work of gaining all the knowledge and certifications needed to become financial coaches themselves precisely because it is so satisfying. They see the level of impact they can have coaching, and it becomes a key part of living their purpose, which is the last module in the START™ framework.

To see the impact of intentional role modeling, all you have to do is look at the story of our company, which has managed to impact millions of financial lives, with a staff of just 25 financial coaches! The reason for this level of impact is what I call the "ripple effect" that comes from intentional role modeling. When we coach people, more often than not, they pass those lessons onto others, along with the recommendation to work with one of our financial coaches, including our Virtual Financial Coach, Aimee. If one person impacts five people, and those five people each go on to impact an additional five and so on, it's not long before the result is the financial transformation of a workforce or a community! It's very difficult, as an individual person, to fully appreciate this chain of events, but we've seen it happen over and over in the 23 years of our work offering financial coaching as an employee benefit. And because we've seen it so many times, we've actually changed our financial coaching programs to include intentional role modeling, finding creative ways for employees who are comfortable sharing their stories to do so—through podcasts, videos, blog posts, and even workshops and webcasts that our planners conduct. Without the impact of role modeling, our services wouldn't have reached nearly as many people as we have, nor would they have had the same level of impact.

It's one thing to hear from an expert. But it resonates on a whole other level when someone facing a challenge hears from a peer who has gone through the same thing and comes through it much stronger financially than ever could have been imagined. Coaches provide the guidance and accountability needed for people to implement the changes they need to make to their finances, but role models do something arguably more important—they show others what is possible.

EXERCISE

■ What type of intentional role modeling do you plan to pursue? Circle all that apply:

- Broad

- Group

- 1x1

■ What financial challenges did you overcome prior to picking up this book, and what are the lessons you learned that could be beneficial to others, as well as being important to reinforce for yourself?

■ What actions have you already taken as a result of reading this book? Have any of them already improved your finances or reduced your financial stress? Are there important lessons and insights you've learned from taking these steps that you feel would benefit others (and also help you sustain and build upon the progress you've already made)?

14

RAISING FINANCIALLY SUCCESSFUL KIDS

There is one exception to having a choice of whether or not you want to intentionally role model positive financial habits and behaviors, and that is when you are raising children. If you don't have children, you can skip this chapter, unless you have a desire to be a role model for children or provide guidance to parents who are looking for tips around how to teach their children about money—similar to what Jen did when she decided to volunteer at her local youth center.

If you do have children, read on, as this is probably the most important and impactful financial role modeling you will do—something that, if every parent did, would massively change the trajectory of our future.

Many economists are predicting that children and young adults today (members of Gen Z and Generation Alpha, born from 1997 through 2022) will face downward mobility, meaning that they will likely have a less comfortable financial lifestyle than their parents, earning less income (adjusted for inflation) and having a harder time building wealth as a result. In recent years, wages have not kept up with inflation. That means the same paycheck has less purchasing power, and all signs, at least today, point to this continuing. Students today are graduating with record levels of student loan debt, only to discover the degree they got is figuratively and literally not paying off based on the salaries they make coming out of school and for a while into their careers.

This dynamic may change due to supply and demand—between lower birth rates and parents and children deciding that it's simply not worth going into high levels of debt to attain a college degree. However, children today are likely to face higher taxes, more economic and market uncertainty, and far less employment stability than their parents—so even if our children aren't lamenting their student loan debt in the next 10 to 15 years, they are facing headwinds that are going to make it more important than ever that we as parents equip them to be as financially savvy as possible going into adulthood.

The great news is that effective financial role modeling, coupled with intentionally taking the time to teach your children about money, can have a significant impact on their financial success as adults. Below is a summary of the latest research on this topic:

- Parents who intentionally role model good financial habits and behaviors for their children are much more likely to set their children up to have significantly more comfortable financial lives than their parents had.
- A recent study by researchers at Brigham Young University found that the benefits of intentionally role modeling positive financial habits and behaviors for children extended well beyond setting their children up for success financially, and actually impacted the quality of their relationships as adults, most notably with their spouses and significant others.[1] It turns out that children who have parents who taught them strong money management skills end up developing the high levels of self-esteem needed to sustain positive relationships with others!

So the question now becomes, what is the best way to do this? How can you be the best possible financial role model for your children? What is the best way to impart critical financial lessons that will set them up for success as an adult? What is the best way to set them on a path of upward mobility, where they have the wherewithal to overcome the financial challenges facing their generation and actually achieve financial freedom even faster than you and your parents were able to?

To answer these questions, I have both general recommendations, based on hundreds of studies on what has been most effective, and specific recommendations. My goal is to help you tailor a plan based on the unique needs of your children, recognizing that each child is different in terms of how they learn, and what they need to integrate those lessons into their psyches and their behavior in order to become financially successful adults.

First, the general recommendations:

- **Openly discuss your finances with your children in an age-appropriate way.** Many parents feel that it is inappropriate to share their financial circumstances with their children, especially if they are financially struggling. Instinctually, we want to shield our children from anything we think might be upsetting or stressful. However, the reality is that children are smarter than we think, and once they reach school age, they generally pick up on what's going on regardless of whether we are open about our financial struggles or not. It turns out that financial challenges, contrary to what we might intuitively believe, can be incredibly useful learning experiences for children. According to a study by T. Rowe Price, children who are aware their parents declared bankruptcy are more than twice as likely than those who are unaware to say they are smart about money.[2] Children benefit more when parents take the time to discuss their financial struggles, sharing the lessons they learned and changes they've made as a result, than when these challenges are hidden. The study also found that parents who discussed financial topics with their kids at least once a week were significantly more likely to have children who said they were smart about money (64 percent versus 41 percent).

■ **Set up a system to provide your children with the chance to manage their own money on an ongoing basis.** This gives them the experience of understanding the responsibilities associated with having money, so they learn important lessons about spending and saving money early on, and establish a healthy relationship with money. Children who receive a weekly allowance or who earn money for doing chores are also much more likely to have better money habits as adults, with the following habits being the most notable, based on the same T. Rowe Price study mentioned above:

- **Saving money instead of spending it.** Only 40 percent of those who have the chance to manage their own money spend it as soon as they get it versus 53 percent who didn't have the chance to manage their own money.

- **Being honest about what they spend their money on.** Only 29 percent of children who managed their own money reported lying to their parents about how they spent it versus 49 percent who didn't have the chance to manage their own money.

- **Having less entitlement about money.** Only 52 percent of children who managed their own money expected their parents to buy them whatever they wanted versus 65 percent of those who didn't have the chance to manage their own money expected this.

- **Feeling less shame about money.** Only 30 percent of children who managed their own money reported feeling ashamed for having less than their peers versus 50 percent who didn't have the chance to manage their own money.

■ **Ensure that you practice what you preach when it comes to money.** This may have the most important impact, with most studies finding that it's what we do, not what we say to our children, when it comes to money that matters most.

■ **Keep in mind that your children not only pick up on how you manage your money, but recognize the relationship you have**

to it—namely, your money script. Children are little sponges, and the way we react to financial situations or decisions impacts them deeply. It's important for everyone to develop a positive money script, but there's an added level of importance if you are a parent, because it's not only your life that will be impacted by your money script but the lives of your children. You don't want to unintentionally teach your children that money is associated with stress or anxiety, or even worse, defeatism—that feeling that you will never get ahead because you are "bad at money" or "the cards are stacked against you" because of how you grew up or the situation you are in. On the other end of the spectrum, you don't want your children to learn that money represents their worth because you show more respect to people who have money than to those who don't. And you certainly don't want them to be in a state of denial or complacency because you ignored your own money challenges, with the attitude that "money comes and money goes" and there's no reason to pay much attention to it at all. Instead you'll want to pass on a healthy money script, which includes the following tenets:

- **No one is naturally "good" or "bad" with money.** Financial success comes first and foremost from how you think about and manage your money on a daily basis, but it also comes from the way you react to setbacks or go about planning for major financial goals. Here you'll want to make sure you are intentional in the way you manage your money, handle financial challenges, and plan for your future, with a positive mindset that shows your children that you always control what you can, and use setbacks as an opportunity to learn and improve.

- **Money is fuel for ultimately building the life you want to live, and should be used accordingly.** Here it's important to make sure that you are spending money in a way that provides the best possible life for yourself and your family, giving them opportunities they wouldn't otherwise have, as opposed to getting caught up in the status aspect of money, where you are always trying to keep up with or exceed your peers for the sake of appearances.

- **Life is unpredictable, and you will face setbacks and challenges.** The best you can do is make sure you have taken steps to bulletproof your finances, so you are prepared when a problem occurs.

- **You are going to make mistakes with money.** We all do. The important thing is not to beat yourself up over them, but to use your mistakes as an opportunity to learn so you can do better the next time. Mistakes are not permanent, nor are they shameful; and if you learn from them, they will actually make you stronger.

PUTTING THIS INTO PRACTICE—BASED ON YOUR CHILDREN'S UNIQUE NEEDS

The above recommendations are good practices for virtually all parents, once their children are at the maturity level to understand the concept of money. However, through all the coaching we've done with people who are parents, and in some cases with their children as well, we've discovered that beyond these best practices is the fundamental understanding that applies to parenting in general—that every child is unique.

To really maximize children's chances of financial success, you must tailor the financial lessons and experiences you provide them to their specific needs. For example, if children are very precocious and independent, it's better to give them a little more freedom, but with a combination of incentives and boundaries that keep them on track; you might match dollars they give and save, or reduce their allowance if they don't manage their money responsibly. Other children may need more structure. They will benefit more if you require them to save a certain amount, and give them guidelines about what they can and cannot spend their money on.

Here are some guidelines to help you determine the best possible way to teach your children about money, based on their unique personalities:

- **Consider your children's personality and maturity level.** Determine the following:

  - **How much they can process and understand when it comes to money.** You will want to challenge your children and expand their thinking, but not to the point where you are confusing or intimidating them. Children go from understanding money in concept—as something that they can trade for goods or services—to understanding the value of currency (a penny, nickel, dime, quarter, dollar, and so on), to having a good understanding of what different things cost, to understanding the trade-offs associated with money and the ways it can be used. At the highest level of maturity, they understand business and economic concepts associated with money—the difference between an expense and an investment, for example. As a parent, you'll want to make sure that when you talk about money, you are talking at their level of understanding and expanding it progressively, but at a pace that works for them.

  - **Their ability to emotionally handle conversations about money.** While the T. Rowe Price study showed that children who knew about things like their parents' bankruptcy fared better financially in life than those who were shielded from it, it's obviously not appropriate to have a long financial talk about all your financial challenges with a five-year-old child, even if the child happens to be intellectually precocious enough to understand what you are talking about. What, when, and how you share should be tailored to your child's emotional readiness. If you have a child who is highly sensitive, anxious, or easily overwhelmed, you'll want to share the information more slowly (especially if it is negative information), so your child has a chance to process it in a healthy way. As well, you'll want to reassure your child that you have a plan and everything will be OK. If appropriate, share your plans with your child so your child will know that things are under control. If your financial setback is a result of a mistake you made, share what the mistake was, what you've learned, and how you are going to do better so it won't happen again. It's important for all children, but particularly for sensitive children, to understand that people make mistakes, but that you can emerge stronger and smarter if you learn the lesson from your mistake. In terms of proactively sharing things like how you are budgeting, saving, and investing, take this in steps regardless of your child's temperament, to gauge how your child is learning and responding.

- **The degree of help or structure they need managing their own money.** Some children learn best by experiencing things themselves, even if that means failing; and absent that, all the rules and structure in the world won't have an impact on how they actually manage their money in adulthood. I was that way as a child—I had to learn on my own in order to figure out how to modify my behavior. Other children crave structure for how they should spend, save, and invest their money and will carry whatever structure you provide into adulthood. Still others may need a middle-of-the-road approach, where they have more structure to start with and then are given more latitude over time, in order to develop strong money habits. Before you decide to take a "hands-on" or "hands-off" approach with respect to setting up structure around any allowance you give them, think about their personality first and foremost so you put a system in place that will maximize their chances of cultivating good money habits that carry into adulthood.

■ **Consider your children's strengths and weaknesses and how those translate to money, with the goal of helping your children leverage their strengths and mitigate their**

weaknesses. I hate it when people say that they or their children are "bad with money," because money is so complex, in terms of all the things you need to do to successfully manage it, that it defies logic to make such a sweeping statement. The vast majority of people, and by extension, the vast majority of kids, are exceptional with money in certain areas, good with it in others, and challenged by it in others.

Your children are not born "good" or "bad" with money; they have natural strengths and weaknesses that show up in the way they innately manage their money. Think about your children's greatest strengths and conversely their weaknesses as you determine the best way to teach them about money and how much latitude to give them in managing their own. If they are anxious by nature, they may actually be excellent savers but unable to make purchasing decisions without overanalyzing even the smallest things. Your job is to encourage the saving, but help them understand that it's not productive to drive to nine different stores to find the "perfect" item. Their time and yours has a value, and neither of you can get that time back. That is an important lesson for them to learn as they become adults.

Conversely, when children are impulsive and prone to spending, help them take a step back and think about everything they want that they won't be able to buy if they spend their money in the spur of the moment. But praise their decisiveness. Knowing what you want is important—and that is a trait that will benefit them both financially and other ways in life—as long as they take the time to make sure they aren't acting rashly.

■ **Watch your children's natural money habits so you can nurture their positive habits and help them change their negative habits.** My son, from an early age, has always been a giver when it comes to money—normally a very honorable trait. However, when he was in preschool, he gave away his birthday money to kids who didn't get money for their birthday—a noble gesture to be sure, but those parents had reasons for not giving their children money and didn't appreciate Jay giving money to their kids. We had to explain that there are better ways to give to people in need, and that it was OK for him to keep some of the money he had for things he wanted, because as an adult, he will have to support himself and likely a family.

Jay is now a teenager and caught up in investing his money, which again is a good habit. However, he's drawn to investing in cryptocurrency and trading stocks on Robinhood, both of which entail taking way too much risk if he continues this into adulthood. We've had to talk to him about the concept of risk and the fact that just because he may have had success with a handful of "short squeezes" (don't get me started with Gamestop!) does not mean the odds are in his favor long term. He has since decided to bucket his money into saving, spending, investing, and giving—at least informally—and has a much better perspective on the best way to manage his money.

■ **Pay special attention to your children's money scripts as well as any unusual actions with respect to money.** One of our financial coaches caught her five-year-old son stealing money from her wallet. He is an incredibly kind, loyal, empathic child with an overdeveloped sense of fairness and a strong moral compass even at his young age. She was shocked when she caught him in action, and her natural impulse was to discipline him. Fortunately, she stopped herself and asked him why he was stealing her money. She was shocked again, this time by his answer. It turns out he was worried that "Mommy didn't have enough money," and he wanted to help her by saving some of her money for her. She asked him why he thought she didn't have enough money, and he answered, "When I ask you in the store if you will buy me a toy, you always say that we can't afford it."

What his mom was actually intending to communicate was "Honey, you have enough toys to play with, and it would be foolish to spend this much money on another toy when you have so many at home you don't even use." She short-cut that message to "We can't afford it," and he was left with the impression that she didn't have "enough money." Be very mindful of the words you use when you react to money situations in front of your children. They pick up much more than you think, and ultimately the things you say and do become part of the money scripts that drive their behavior as adults.

NOTE

Know that if you have multiple children, it can be considerably harder to have separate rules for each child. In this case, the best thing to do is let all your children know what you expect from them when it comes to how they learn about and manage their money. If one child learns the basics of money very quickly, and shows he or she is ready for more autonomy, you can then explain why he or she has earned this privilege, and what your other children can do to earn the same privilege. As your children get older, you can even share that your job as a parent is to raise them in a way that enables them to be the best version of themselves, and equips them to suc-ceed as adults, which means parenting each of them in a way that is best for them in the long run. You are likely to get an eye roll, but that doesn't mean they aren't listening. Think back to how much your parents impacted you—you have a similar level of impact on your children even if it may not seem like it in the moment.

EXERCISE

Make a plan around how to role model good financial habits and behaviors for your children, as well as intentionally teach them how to best manage their money so they are set up for success as adults.

1. For each child, determine whether or not he or she is old enough to participate in discussions about how you—and your spouse/partner if you have a dual-parent household—are budgeting, spending, saving, and investing your money.

2. Determine the best way to do this that fits with your family's way of life. For me and my son, it's a combination of regular meetings and organic conversations that come up either through his asking questions or my intentionally sharing why we are making specific financial decisions and what we hope to gain from them.

3. Decide how you are going to provide your children with the ability to manage their own money—for example, giving them a small allowance (even if it's tiny, it makes a difference), paying them for chores, or, as they get older, encouraging them to find a way to earn money through their own part-time jobs or entrepreneurial ventures.

4. Determine how you are going to approach teaching your children about saving and investing. Decide how flexible you want to be in terms of letting them save, spend, or invest their own money, based on what you feel will yield the best result. To create a plan you can put in motion sooner rather than later, determine (1) whether you are going to share your guidance but ultimately let them do what they want, knowing they will learn from their mistakes, (2) incentivize certain behaviors (e.g., matching what they save), or (3) put parameters around what they do with their money (e.g., requiring they save at least 10 to 20 percent in a separate savings or investment account they cannot touch until they are an adult)? All children are different,

and age comes into play here. If your children are older and more mature and tend to learn quickly, it's generally best to give them more freedom. For younger children or children that have a hard time delaying gratification, parameters are much more important.

Module 5

THRIVE BY LIVING YOUR PURPOSE

ABOUT THIS MODULE

So now we come to the end of the START™ framework—the capstone of it all—and the most important thing that money can buy: *the ability to live your purpose*.

The dictionary definition of purpose is "the reason for which something is done or created, or the reason for which it exists." Without getting overly spiritual, whether you believe in God or fate or anything larger than yourself or whether you simply want to make the most of your time on earth, you likely want your life to have meaning that transcends your own wants and needs. That meaning—that reason you exist—is your purpose, and the closer you are able to get to it, the more fulfilling your life will be.

Financially, finding your purpose means finding your "true north"—the ultimate reason you are doing the work to become financially independent in the first place. When you find it, it becomes the one thing you can always come back to when things get really tough, the motivation to stay the course when you feel discouraged or are having a hard time resisting the urge to make impulsive financial decisions.

In that sense, finding your purpose can fuel your financial success as much as financial success can give you the money to live your purpose. And when both come together, you will be able to do the work you want to do, as opposed to the work you have to do, and say no to anything that doesn't align with your purpose. You will be able to invest more in your most important relationships because you will have the ability to use your most valuable resource—your time—as you see fit. And you will be able to achieve those things on your bucket list that you never thought possible—those things that enrich your life and the lives of those around you—without having to worry about the impact on your finances.

In this module you'll learn how your choices and opportunities expand as you progress financially, as well as how you can define a purpose and track your progress toward it, so you can keep it top of mind as you go through the hard work of becoming financially independent.

15

HOW FINANCIAL PROGRESS TRANSLATES INTO LIVING YOUR TRUE "BEST LIFE"

Most people we coach understand innately that as they progress financially, they will have more choices in life, and less restrictions that compromise their quality and enjoyment of life. What they don't realize is how powerful the connection is. In this chapter, we'll dig into all the areas where money expands your choices and allows you to pursue a much more satisfying, fulfilling, and meaningful life.

To show the incredible impact money has on expanding the choices you have in life, and freeing you from having to make compromises you don't want to make, let's go through the four financial categories we've used throughout the book (suffering, struggling, planning, and optimizing) to examine exactly how this works, using the story of an actual person we coached, Daryl. Daryl progressed through all four categories and transformed his life in the process.

FINANCIALLY SUFFERING

If you are financially suffering—meaning you are dealing with a serious financial crisis that compromises your ability to have safe housing, food, and childcare (if you have children)—your sole focus, after tapping into any community or government resources, is to earn as much money as you can as quickly as possible! The other components of achieving a purposeful life are crowded out by this one aspect—getting paid so you can get the money to resolve your financial crisis and get back on your feet. And you may not even have much choice in what you do or how you do it. If you need to work inhumanely hard—multiple jobs or extra shifts— to bring in the money you need, you will do it. If you need to take a job you hate, but it pays well or will provide you with cash up front, you take it because it will help you resolve the situation faster. If you have to work for a boss that you don't respect, or even like, you do it if that job pays more money than the alternatives.

When Daryl, a 27-year-old distribution center employee, first called us, he definitely fit in the financially suffering category. Daryl was living in his car with his two young boys, after his wife left him and her children, draining all their bank accounts in the process. He was able to use his company's daycare to take care of his boys while he worked, but at night they returned to his car, which was especially concerning given the fact that winter was around the corner and he lived in one of the coldest cities in the country. We were able to connect him with several employer and community resources to ensure he was able to find housing and other critical resources, which at least gave him a degree of relief. However, he didn't feel his housing situation was sustainable long term because he wanted a better life for his children, in a safer neighborhood.

Daryl was fortunate to have an employer who had a compassion fund, and was able to provide him a grant for childcare so he could work nights, knowing his kids were taken care of. He worked the graveyard shift at a manufacturing facility, returned home to get a few hours of sleep and get his kids ready for daycare, and then did the routine all over again. Life was miserable for several months, until he amassed enough for a deposit on a better apartment and was able to move the boys into a safer neighborhood. Once he accomplished that, he was able to secure a better paying, less stressful day job at the distribution center that allowed him to spend more quality time with his kids, moving from the suffering category into the struggling category.

But the financial stress wasn't over. Daryl was making ends meet at that point, but he still had debts to pay off, and he had very little savings to fall back on if something were to go wrong.

FINANCIALLY STRUGGLING

If you are financially struggling—meaning you are not in a financial crisis, you are managing to make ends meet, but you are still struggling with debt and little or no savings—your choices in how you spend your time expand a bit. While you may not be able to leave your current job without securing a new one, you don't have that same level of desperation where you are willing to take any job to make ends meet or have to work multiple jobs to avoid being evicted. You also have a little more bandwidth mentally to focus on your future, because you aren't in that state of crisis that narrows your focus to whatever it takes to survive.

You can begin to think about what you need to do to progress toward the life you want, such as reducing expenses or working at a second job that you can actually tolerate in order to pay down high interest rate debt and build an emergency savings fund so you have more flexibility to make choices that are more aligned with your values and what you truly want out of life. If you have aspirations beyond what your current job will provide, you will want to secure another job before leaving your current one. The good thing is, you'll have more time and mind space to look for a better job. You'll also have more time and the ability to be more present for your family and friends, as you won't be laser-focused on making sure you keep your home and keep food on the table, and you won't be consumed by worrying about your family's health and well-being.

Keep in mind that financially struggling—where 65 percent of Americans are right now—is no picnic. You are always one emergency away from a financial crisis—and living on edge knowing that. But it's significantly better than living in your car and or working harrowing hours to afford a safe place to live for yourself and your children or other loved ones.

At the point where Daryl found better housing in a safe neighborhood, he moved out of a state of financial crisis and into the struggling category. At this point, he was no longer exhausted from his crazy workweek and was able to spend quality time during weekends with his boys. He took them to church to instill a sense of community and stability into their lives, and took them with him when he volunteered at the homeless shelter in his neighborhood, serving food to those who weren't fortunate enough to have a home. This was something deeply important to him, having gone through the financial crisis he had faced. Although Daryl didn't know it yet, he was already starting to live his purpose by giving back to others, including giving his children whatever opportunities he could provide them.

As most people who face financial crisis are, Daryl was bound and determined never to end up in the situation he was in again. He began working more often with his financial coach to figure out what he could do to further improve his finances, so that he would be better equipped to weather any financial setbacks that came his way. He was still quite stressed, losing sleep over the thought of something going wrong to put him back to where he had been, in a car in the cold with his two boys.

But the stress motivated him, and he worked on a plan to set up an emergency fund and then pay off credit card debts that he and his wife had incurred during their marriage. The emergency fund was critical in his mind, because it meant he would have something to fall back on, and he decided he wanted to save up a full six months of living expenses. He and his coach set up an automatic transfer of 30 percent of his income from his paycheck to a separate savings account to be used for emergencies, and within a year and a half, he had achieved his goal of six months of living expenses saved in case something were to go wrong. At the same time, he began to get to know his coworkers at the distribution center better, and he became more interested in what he could do to help them improve their lives and working conditions.

The head of the distribution center took notice and offered Daryl a promotion—as manager of his team. The previous manager had left, and Daryl was the obvious choice for a replacement, based on the way he took care of the other employees and made sure they had what they needed to succeed. Again, his purpose of giving back was taking hold—this time manifesting itself at work. The promotion, coupled with a surprise bonus for improving the team's morale and productivity, got him into a position where he was able to ultimately eliminate his high interest rate credit card debt by consolidating his debt to a lower interest rate card. At the same time, he redirected the 30 percent of his paycheck that previously had gone into his savings account for emergencies, applying it now to his credit card balance. Within another year, he was out of credit card debt entirely and ready to begin planning for his future.

PLANNING

As you become financially stable, meaning you have your emergency fund in place and aren't weighed down by high levels of debt, you will be able to begin saving and investing more for your future, including having a greater financial cushion should you want to make more significant life changes. At this stage, you may be able to quit a job you don't like without worrying as much about having an offer in hand from a new employer (though it's always best to do so if you can), and you can focus more time on making sure you are working toward a career you truly love. You can explore educational or career development opportunities for yourself (just make sure you take full advantage of what your employer offers in this area). You also can begin to donate some of your time and money to worthy causes without feeling like you are breaking the bank or worrying about jeopardizing your employment in the process. And if you are so inclined, you may be able to help out family members who are in need, so they can progress financially and reap the same benefits you have.

If you have children, you'll be able to spend even more quality time with them because you'll likely have more control over your work hours and also have less financial stress that keeps you from being present. You'll be able to afford better educational and enrichment experiences for your children, so they are better prepared to succeed in life, and you can do things like taking more frequent family vacations or providing other experiences that will give them lifelong memories.

When Daryl reached this stage, three years after living in his car with his boys, he decided he wanted to save for a home of his own. Now that he had all his credit card debt paid off, he was in significantly better shape. As a result, he was able to take the 30 percent of his paycheck that had automatically gone to pay off his credit card and reallocate that money to a money market account to save for a down payment on a home, as well as allocating bonuses for this. He also decided to invest 6 percent of his salary into his 401(k) to take advantage of his employer's dollar-for-dollar match, making his annual investment around 12 percent, in line with what most financial planners recommend. Better yet, this only cost him 4 percent of his salary when you factor in the tax deduction he was getting; 401(k) contributions go in pretax, reducing your taxable income by the amount you contribute annually!

Daryl and his boys were still living on a relatively tight budget, given Daryl's desire to focus on the future as opposed to spending in the present, but he was able to have enough to enroll the boys in soccer and karate—both sports he felt passionate about for the skills they taught—teamwork with soccer and discipline with karate.

Daryl was also able to take the role of lead volunteer at the homeless shelter. Similar to what happened at work, other volunteers looked to him as a mentor and role model, a natural leader, someone who inspired them to be their best. Again, his purpose of giving back was coming out.

At this point, Daryl started to think of himself differently. He realized all he had accomplished to provide a better life for himself, his children, the employees he managed, and the homeless people he helped in the shelter; and he felt deeply fulfilled by not only his accomplishments but the impact he was having. He started to talk to his coach about wanting to get into a financial position where he could make a bigger impact, though he didn't yet know exactly what that looked like. But what he *did* know was that it would take a greater level of financial independence to be able to achieve that.

OPTIMIZING

When you enter the optimizing category, you are well on your way to financial independence: You have a plan in place to achieve your most important financial goals in the time frame you desire, and you have a significant nest egg that provides both the financial latitude and emotional comfort needed to prioritize what you want professionally over what you have to do. Suddenly you can take a job you love without worrying so much about the compensation—a job that makes you excited to get out of bed in the morning and gives you a tremendous sense of fulfillment, one that makes each Monday a day you look forward to rather than simply tolerating, or worse, dreading. And if your dream job is not available at your current employer, you can take time out of the workforce to find that job—because you have the financial cushion to leave your job if it's not the right job for you without first getting another job. You also can expand your investment in personal and career development opportunities, and even begin to cross off some of the things on your bucket list, things that you've always wanted to do but never could afford.

If you have children, you can also expand the opportunities you give them. If they would benefit from additional education or enrichment because they have specific talents or needs, you can ensure they have access to the best resources—say, private schooling, tutoring in their areas of interest or areas where they need additional help, or other activities that will expand their horizons and give them important life skills. You also can begin to look into philanthropy—donating more intentionally and on a larger scale to the causes that are most important to you. And you can spend more on once-in-a-lifetime experiences that your family will cherish as incredible memories for the rest of their lives—knowing that you have the financial wherewithal to do so without derailing your goals.

Five years later, Daryl moved from the planning category into the optimizing category. At this point, he was not fully financially independent, but he had built a good-sized nest egg. The equity in his home significantly increased, because he had bought his home in a neighborhood that was up and coming and real estate prices were soaring. He was on track for retirement, now contributing 11 percent to his 401(k), thanks to using his employer's annual auto-escalator feature, which automatically increased his contributions to his 401(k) by 1 percent a year (less than the merit increase he received annually). He had a very strong emergency savings fund (given what he went through, he wanted to get to 12 months of living expenses—more than most planners recommend but critical to his peace of mind). And he had opened and funded 529 accounts to save for his boys' college educations.

Now he was able to turn his attention more to what he truly wanted to do with his life—which was to help others in need, people who were facing financial crises similar to what he had faced. As much as he did love managing his team and got a lot of satisfaction from helping them grow and develop their skills and secure much-deserved promotions, he wanted to do more. He thought back to his employer's compassion fund, which provided him the grant for childcare so he could work nights. After talking to his financial coach, he decided to reach out to the executive director of the compassion fund and inquire about open positions. It turns out she did have an opening for an intake counselor, and she felt he had both the real-life experience and skill set to do the job, but the salary was less than what he was currently making. He'd be taking a pay cut of about 20 percent. After all the work he did to get his finances in order, he was worried about moving backward; but when he and his financial coach crunched the numbers, it turned out he was in strong enough financial shape to be able to make the new situation work without jeopardizing his other goals. He took the job, and he absolutely loved it!

Between his new role at his employer's compassion fund, his work at the homeless shelter, and his job as a parent mentoring his boys, he was the happiest and most fulfilled he'd ever been. This of course made him a better employee, father, and volunteer—and created a ripple effect that impacted many more lives than even he realized.

EXERCISE

1. What are the lessons from Daryl's story that really resonated with you, and how can you apply them to your own life?

2. What financial category are you in right now—suffering, struggling, planning, or optimizing?

3. Provided you are not suffering or in a financial crisis, what can you do now to begin to pursue things that provide you with a greater sense of fulfillment, and if you have children, provide them with more opportunities to develop the skills necessary to have successful lives as adults?

4. As you progress through the different financial categories, how do you plan to use your greater levels of financial independence to increase your sense of fulfillment?

16

LIVING YOUR PURPOSE

Coming off the last chapter, you might be thinking that simply having the freedom to live life on your own terms—which is what increases as you progress toward financial independence—is enough for a happy, fulfilling life. You may be wondering, "What's with all this focus on purpose? What if I'm happy simply building the life I want for myself and my family, and having the time to do the things I enjoy?"

The answer, I think, lies in a misconception that many people have about purpose. No one is expecting you to become Mother Teresa, or to dedicate your life 24/7 to a single cause. The entire point of having a purpose is to enhance your life's satisfaction, not to create a burden you somehow have to live up to because you have this grandiose sense of what purpose means—some sort of obligation to change the world or improve the future of all humanity. To put it more bluntly, there is no purpose to having a purpose if it doesn't serve you first and foremost.

When you remove any sort of pressure associated with the concept of "purpose" and instead focus on what gives you the greatest sense of fulfillment, you give yourself the freedom to have a purpose that feels right to you, and everything becomes clearer. For many people we coach, their purpose is to simply be a positive influence on the people they love, because making their loved ones happy makes them happy. There's no right or wrong answer to the question, "What is your purpose?" (Well, provided your purpose doesn't harm anyone else!) And only you have the answer. This chapter is designed to help you find and define your purpose so you can figure out how to take more steps to live your purpose as you improve your finances, similar to the way Daryl did.

Figure 16.1 is a diagram, developed by our financial coaches, to help you find your purpose, based on the intersection of four key areas: what you love to do; what you are good at doing; what you feel the world needs—in other words, where you want to make an impact; and until you are financially independent, what meets those criteria but also pays the bills.

FIGURE 16.1   Find your purpose.

Let's start with what you love to do, because that typically feeds all the other areas that help to clarify your purpose. There may be a lot of things that fit into this category, ranging from reading a great book, to playing practical jokes on your friends, to doing sports like skiing or boating, to engaging in hobbies like painting or woodworking, and these are certainly things you should continue doing. But in most cases, they are not necessarily connected to finding your purpose. When we talk about "what you love to do" in terms of finding your purpose, the key is to find the things that provide you with the *most enduring* level of joy and fulfill-ment versus a temporary rush that feels exhilarating but quickly fades and leaves you without any real sense of accomplishment or meaning.

Those who have researched purpose often talk about the impor-tance of going back to your childhood to find out what gives you that enduring level of joy and fulfillment. That's because as kids without adult responsibilities, unburdened by the expectations society places on us as we mature, we naturally gravitate toward doing the things that provide us enduring joy.

In my case, I loved babysitting, tutoring, and leading the neighbor-hood kids in a steady string of creative pursuits, from starting a neigh-borhood newspaper to performing dance extravaganzas (google Deney Terrio) for an audience of parents forced to stop what they were doing to watch our theatrics. There was even an ill-fated "neighborhood Olympics," which we had the audacity to sell tickets to, only to have my dad cancel after one kid almost ran headfirst into a wall.

On the surface these examples look like three distinctly different pursuits, but once I dug into what exactly I enjoyed about doing these things, common themes became apparent. They were all about taking a leadership role in some form or fashion—something I loved, was good at (neighborhood Olympics and bad dancing aside), and felt was needed in the world. This has played out in my adult life, most notably with running Financial Finesse, but also with the way I choose to mentor my son, and the role I take in my extended family whenever there's a need to make important decisions. My purpose is to use my leadership skills to help people, individually and collectively, to improve their lives for the better.

As you take your own trip down memory lane, write down those things you loved doing and think about why they gave you such a sense of joy and fulfillment, beyond the typical "fun" childhood activities like going to amusement parks, having sleepovers, or getting out of a day of class to go on a field trip. Did you love creative projects where you got to build something entirely new; or was it taking a leadership role and feeling the deep level of satisfaction that comes from getting people on board with a specific idea or plan; or was it, perhaps, participating in team sports where you collaborated with others to achieve a common goal? What were those things that, even as a teenager, you loved to do despite the fact most of your peers would never consider them "fun"?

You will discover that the things you really loved doing probably had the following in common:

1. They gave you a sense of accomplishment—that feeling that you made a difference and had a positive impact on others. As humans, the feeling of satisfaction and fulfillment that comes from accomplishing something we believe truly matters is one of the most meaningful levels of joy we can achieve.

2. They put you in a state of what famed psychologist and author Mihaly Csikszentmihalyi calls "flow," where you are so lost in what you are doing that hours pass by without your even realizing it. It is a beautiful feeling, almost like some sort of outside force is guiding you. Some people even liken it to experiencing "divine intervention." When you are in flow, things feel effortless, because you are tapping into your talents at their highest level. You'll hear people in flow say, "*This* is what I'm meant to be doing!" or "This is what I was put on this earth to do!"

Bottom line: If you follow what you love, you will also uncover what you are uniquely talented at and what provides you the greatest sense of accomplishment. This will naturally lead you to your purpose.

DEFINING YOUR PURPOSE

The next step is to very clearly and succinctly define your purpose. The best thing you can do here is to boil your purpose down to a single sentence, based on the reflection you've done to pinpoint the intersection between what you love most, when you are in that state of flow, and what gives you the greatest sense of accomplishment. It can be anything from "Helping people improve their mental health," to "Doing what I can to help those less fortunate," to "Improving the lives of the people I love most." It doesn't have to be perfect, just a starting point to work from. In fact, I recommend you limit the time you spend on this to 30 minutes max. Remember, this is your life, not a graded assignment! No one besides you even needs to know what your purpose is, and you aren't making a lifetime commitment here. You can change it as your life evolves—as you have experiences that broaden your thinking around what you really love or that cause you to uncover talents you didn't know you had.

LIVING YOUR PURPOSE

Now comes the harder part—something Daryl discovered on his own, but you have the opportunity to do proactively—namely, figuring out how to infuse your purpose across the different areas of your life. Obviously, you'll have to start based on where you are today financially, but it doesn't end there. The most important—and arguably most fun—part is planning for what you will be able to do as you progress financially and have more money, time, and mind space to dedicate toward living your purpose.

The best model I've seen to ensure that the key aspects of your life are as aligned as possible to your purpose comes from my industry colleague Kevin Clark, Director of Strategic Growth Initiatives for Marketing, Communications and Partnerships at Intuit. When he shared it with me, I immediately asked if I could share it with our financial coaches to use as part of the coaching process, as well as everyone who reads this book. It's illustrated in Figure 16.2.

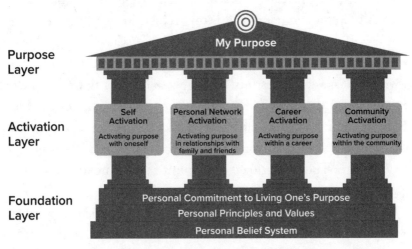

FIGURE 16.2   Kevin J. Clark's Purpose Management Framework™.

I've read a lot about purpose over the years, entire books dedicated to the topic, but most manage to be both complex and abstract at the same time, requiring a huge amount of effort to digest, let alone apply to your own life. Kevin's model is the opposite. Its power is in its simplicity. Without taking you through tedious steps, it gives you an immediate understanding of how your purpose connects to the different areas of your life, and it provides a way to track your progress in each area to ensure you are maximizing your sense of fulfillment in life as you progress financially. Kevin reviews it annually to track his own progress against his purpose, and he recommends others do the same. To date, he's mentored dozens of people using this framework, and the vast majority have changed their lives and their finances for the better as a result.

In Kevin's case, his purpose is to "help individuals and organizations achieve their respective potentials." In his personal life, it has meant supporting his wife in her dream to become partner at the accounting firm she worked for. And it also means helping his children become the best versions of themselves by encouraging them to pursue what they love to do, but also making sure they are learning important life lessons that will set them up for success as adults (including financial literacy, which he considers foundational to this goal). Within his professional network, it means mentoring others to help them achieve their greatest potential. In his career (what he categorizes as his professional life in his model), it means helping company clients, organizations, entrepreneurs and employees discover their respective potentials. This also includes helping the employees he personally manages to reach their greatest potentials, knowing that many are destined for bigger and better things than what they are currently doing, and it's his job to get them there. And last, within his community, he helps fund and lead initiatives for select universities in an effort to help them improve the quality and effectiveness of the mentorship and educational opportunities they provide so students can achieve their greatest potentials.

I use Kevin as an example so you can see how this exercise plays out. My hope is that his model will help you live a more fulfilled, intentional, purposeful life as you achieve increasing levels of financial independence—and, paradoxically, motivate you to do the work to improve your finances so you can devote more time, money, and energy to living your purpose. How you choose to use the model, or for that matter, how you choose to use any of the guidance provided in this book, is entirely up to you.

Only you know what you need to do to create an incredibly fulfilling and deeply satisfying life, and what steps you are willing to take to manage your finances in order to get there. All I ask is that you keep in mind that the real power of money is not the material things it can buy, or the luxury lifestyle it can enable, but the ability it gives you to live the most fulfilling life possible, in your own way, on your own terms. That is truly the life-changing magic of money.

NOTES

Chapter 1

1. http://surveys.associatedpress.com/data/SRBI/AP-AOL%20Health%20Poll%20 Topline%20040808_FINAL_debt%20stress.pdf .
2. https://finhealthnetwork.org/wp-content/uploads/2022/02/Employee-Debt-Report -2022.pdf.
3. https://pubmed.ncbi.nlm.nih.gov/2190480/.

Chapter 4

1. https://www.afcpe.org/news-and-publications/the-standard/2018-3/the-power-of -accountability/.
2. http://www.amazon.com/gp/product/B000FC10GG/?tag=spacforrent-20.
3. You can access the video of the talk at https://www.ucdavis.edu/curiosity-gap/how -do-you-bounce-back-after-setback%C2%A0.
4. https://www.nber.org/papers/w16518.

Chapter 5

1. https://journals.sagepub.com/doi/abs/10.1177/1948550613511499.

Chapter 6

1. https://www.pymnts.com/study/reality-check-paycheck-to-paycheck-high-income -revolving-credit-card-debt-loans.
2. https://magazine.realtor/news-and-commentary/interactive-median-home-price-map.
3. https://www.federalreserve.gov/econresdata/feds/2016/files/2016053pap.pdf.

Chapter 7

1. https://www.healthcarebluebook.com/explore-home/.
2. https://www.nahac.com/find-an-advocate#!directory/map/ord=lnm.
3. http://www.claims.org/.
4. http://www.patientadvocate.org/.
5. https://pirg.org/articles/the-real-price-of-medications/.

Chapter 14

1. https://journals.sagepub.com/doi/abs/10.1177/0192513X211057536?journalCode =jfia.
2. https://www.moneyconfidentkids.com/us/en/news-and-research/research/2017 -parents--kids---money-survey-results.html.

ACKNOWLEDGMENTS

It takes a village to write a book, and behind this book is a movement of people who have dedicated their lives to providing life-changing financial guidance to as many people as possible. On the book side, none of this would have been possible without Michele Matrisciani and Adam Chromy, who reached out to me with the idea of this book and gave me both the freedom to make it my own and the guidance to save me from myself, as well as Patricia Wallenburg for her incredible care and diligence managing the entire process of turning a rough draft into a fully finished book.

I also want to thank my amazing team of planners—Greg Ward, Scott Stark, Erik Carter, Julie Everett, Anita Pippin, and Reynolds Saunders—who spent countless hours helping me research, write, fact-check, and integrate user stories; Laura Chambliss-Stamps for her wise counsel; Maggie Weinberg, my amazing Head of Marketing for her tireless work on getting this ready for publication; and all the Financial Finesse employees who have contributed the blood, sweat, and tears needed not just to create this business, but to pioneer the broader financial coaching industry.

Thank you to Bill Chetney for taking a bet on me and Financial Finesse many years ago and creating an entirely new line of business to bring our services to retirement plan participants. You may never read this book, but you gave me the confidence and inspiration to write it. And J. R. Tolver, thanks for your friendship, partnership, and vision, and for all the work you've done betting on the future of bringing financial education to the next generation. You are making history, and it's inspiring to be a part of it.

To our clients who have brought our financial coaching benefit to their employees and have embedded it into their cultures—you have paved the way for future generations of HR and benefits leaders to build workplaces that honor the credo that "our people are our greatest asset." Thank you for your commitment to your employees, and for doing work that may never be fully appreciated but changes lives every single day.

Most importantly, to the two people who are and always will be my heart, Jay and Joe Casale. I don't have words to thank you properly for all the love, laughter, support, and endless adventures. I could never begin to tell you (at least in the word limit I have here) how much I love you. You've given my life a richness and meaning that I never thought possible.

INDEX

Page numbers followed by *f* and *t* refer to figures and tables, respectively.

ABOUT THE AUTHOR

Liz Davidson is a financial education expert and the founder and CEO of Financial Finesse, the nation's leading provider of unbiased financial wellness coaching as an employee benefit, which helps millions of people build stronger financial futures for themselves and their families. She is the author of *What Your Financial Advisor Isn't Telling You: The 10 Essential Truths You Need to Know About Your Money* and the host of the podcast *Financial Wellness at Work*. She lives in California with her husband, son, four dogs, and two cats. For more information, or to determine if your company has Financial Finesse financial coaching as an employer paid benefit, visit www.financialfinesse.com.